"The Sweet and the Bitter"

"The Sweet and the Bitter"

Death and Dying in J. R. R. Tolkien's

The Lord of the Rings

Amy Amendt-Raduege

The Kent State University Press ⊠ *Kent, Ohio*

Library of Congress Catalog Number 2017016112

ISBN 978-1-60635-305-9

Manufactured in the United States of America

Library of Congress Cataloging-in-Publication Data

Names: Amendt-Raduege, Amy, 1968- author.

Title: "The sweet and the bitter" : death and dying in J. R. R. Tolkien's The lord of
    the rings / Amy Amendt-Raduege.

Description: Kent, Ohio : The Kent State University Press, 2017. | Includes
    bibliographical references and index.

Identifiers: LCCN 2017016112 | ISBN 9781606353059 (pbk. : alk. paper) | ISBN
    9781631012877 (epdf)

Subjects: LCSH: Tolkien, J. R. R. (John Ronald Reuel), 1892-1973. Lord of the rings.
    | Death in literature.

Classification: LCC PR6039.O32 L63215 2017 | DDC 823/.912--dc23

LC record available at https://lccn.loc.gov/2017016112

22 21 20 19 18   5 4 3 2 1

Contents

Preface and

Acknowledgments

Tolkien scholarship has made significant advances since the mid-1970s, due in no small part to the contributions of scholars who were courageous enough to champion the literature that they loved even in the face of a certain established resistance. Classes on Tolkien now abound in American universities, appearing in the syllabuses of such prestigious universities as Duke, Rice, and Purdue; academic journals have devoted whole issues to scholarly examination of Tolkien's works, journals such as *Tolkien Studies* and the online *Journal of Tolkien Research* put the professor in the same professional realm as other major British authors. Tolkien has finally come into his own.

It has been my privilege and delight to participate in the growing scholarly interest in Tolkien's work. Originally, however, I had no idea I would be writing about death and dying. The concept for this book came about from a chance observation by Tom Shippey during a session at the International Medieval Congress at Kalamazoo: no one, he said, has ever made a detailed study of all the ways people die. He happened to be speaking specifically of characters in the Old Norse sagas, but it occurred to me that perhaps such a study could be done for the characters of *The Lord of the Rings*. What seemed to me then a relatively straightforward undertaking turned out to be instead a rich and intricate study, filled not only with moments of dying and attitudes toward death but with the importance of memory, the celebration of heroism and sacrifice, and, above all, the enduring power of hope.

Because there are now so many editions of *The Lord of the Rings* available, I have followed the citing convention proposed by *Tolkien Studies*: volume, book, chapter, page, to make it relatively easy for other scholars to find relevant quotations in their own copies. I used the single-volume edition (exactly the way Tolkien wished it), so I have cited any quotations taken from the preface, introduction, or appendixes as *LR*.

In keeping with Tolkien's precedent, I shall use the term "Men" when referring to human beings in *The Lord of the Rings*. At all other times, I shall use the more inclusive "humans," "humankind," or "humanity." It should be noted, however, that Tolkien's use of "Men" is not automatically exclusive; my sense is that it is a deliberate echo of the Old English *mann,* which becomes "men" in the dative and accusative plural. The term certainly could include women, too, though it must be admitted that in heroic poetry, at least, it rarely did. Perhaps Tolkien sensed that behind the Old English word there must have been a similar asterisk-word that included the entire human race, or maybe he was just adhering to the conventional use of his time. But he was certainly aware of the implications of the word: otherwise Éowyn's rejoinder to the Witch-king's statement would make no sense.

A few other notes on terminology are necessary. First, I have used "cosmology" to indicate Tolkien's conception of how the universe works, "mythology" to denote the evolving corpus of stories themselves, and "legendarium" to indicate the entire collection of written works, including *The Hobbit, The Lord of the Rings, The Silmarillion,* and materials now available through The Histories of Middle-earth edited by Christopher Tolkien. The Silmarillion, unitalicized, is sometimes used as a synonym for the legendarium; *The Silmarillion* indicates the collection of stories published under that title.

Hobbit *The Hobbit.* New York: Ballantine, 1966.
   LR *The Lord of the Rings.* New York: Houghton Mifflin, 1994.
   FR *Fellowship of the Ring.*
   TT *The Two Towers*
   RK *The Return of the King*

Silm   *The Silmarillion*. 1977. Boston: Houghton Mifflin, 1998.
UT   *Unfinished Tales*. Boston: Houghton Mifflin, 1980

Tolkien was a medievalist by training and by inclination, and it is now widely recognized how much his professional vocation influenced his private avocation. His profound knowledge of Old English and Old Norse naturally found its way into his writing, and it is sometimes necessary to offer those texts in these languages as a means of enhancing a modern reader's understanding of *The Lord of the Rings*. Unless noted, all translations are my own, and any mistakes therein are likewise my own. Since my interest is primarily in Tolkien's interpretation and application of these texts rather than their precise literal translations, I leave the endless fascination of these stories for the reader to explore.

One of the great advantages of writing a book about death is that it highlights for the author the things she values most about life. My study of Tolkien's theme has emphasized for me the deep and abiding belief that what matters most in life is our interconnectedness with other people. This project owes its success to a variety of people who have helped and supported me during the long journey from the door where it began. The community of Tolkien scholars welcomed me with open arms and took me seriously, even when it seemed as if no one else did. These amazing people probably did not even know they were doing it, but their words of kindness and faith meant more to me than I will ever be able to express. For that reason, I wish to thank Verlyn Flieger, Robin Anne Reid, Bradford Eden, John Howe, Jane Chance, and John R. Holmes. Also deserving of special mention are Mike Foster and Douglas A. Anderson, both of whom gave me encouragement, advice, tips on where to find obscure information, and a much-needed kick in the pants. Finally, I wish to honor the late Diane Hoeveler, my dissertation advisor. Her words of wisdom continue to provide hope and guidance to my students, just as they once did for me.

Writing this project required hours upon hours spent in the Marquette University Archives, during which time I was aided and supported by Susan Stawicki-Vrobel and Matt Blessing. I also owe a great deal to my beta readers, Lisa DePauw Fischer, Kerry Olivetti, and Carol Klees-Starks.

These women were unfailingly supportive, laughed with me, cried with me, listened to me rant, and shared my frustrations and triumphs. Similarly, my parents, Peg and Dick Amendt, and my brother and sister-in-law, Paul and Tamara, listened when I needed a sounding board, and they steadfastly believed in me throughout this process.

Editors rarely get the credit they deserve, but Erin Holman was wonderful. I hardly know where to begin. This book would not be what it is without her. Her sense of humor and meticulous attention to detail reminded me why I write and teach in the first place. Way to go, Erin.

And finally, I come last to those who are first in my thoughts: my wonderful family. My husband, John, and my three wonderful children, Andrew, Alexandra, and Ariana, believed in me, took on extra chores, tried very hard to minimize the in-fighting, and learned to sort their own laundry. You are the greatest. I am profoundly grateful that I have been given the opportunity to do what I love, but it wouldn't mean anything without you four. *Lux et veritas et comedia.*

Introduction

On December 28, 2004, Staff Sergeant Dustin C. Holcomb wrote a letter honoring his commanding officer, Captain William W. Jacobsen. The letter began not with a commendation of his officer's rapport with his men, his bravery, or even of Jacobsen's status as a hero, though all those qualities are mentioned later. Instead, he started with a simple reminiscence of the moment of recognition that initiates friendship: their shared appreciation of J. R. R. Tolkien's epic fantasy *The Lord of the Rings:*

> He was inspecting the barracks before signing for the building. He came to my room and noticed that I was a fan of *The Lord of the Rings.* He did his inspection quickly and then started talking about the movies and books. We visited for 10–15 minutes, during which I told him that I was disappointed that we were supposed to leave for Iraq before the extended edition of the third movie was available. He told me that he had asked his wife to send it to him as soon as she could and that when he got it we would have a movie marathon.[1]

The marathon never happened. Captain Jacobsen was killed by a suicide bomber just before Christmas.

Like many soldiers deployed throughout the world, Holcomb and Jacobsen carried the text of *The Lord of the Rings* with them. Though at least one soldier described the book as "a workout both mentally and physically," copies of the text have been reported at battlefields and bunkers, patrols and palaces, fronts and foxholes.[2] At just under 1,140 pages, the paperback edition weighs in at 2 lbs., 7.5 oz.—added to the eighty pounds of equipment the average soldier already carries. These soldiers are caught in the midst of a very real conflict, daily confronted with horror, suffering, and death. Yet they choose to read, repeatedly, a fairy-story built not on weapons of mass destruction or high-tech weaponry or even everyday life but an imagined past where the most advanced weapons are swords, the cavalry is a cavalry and not a cavalcade of tanks, and the old heroic code is a lived experience.[3]

For all its fantastic trappings, then, *The Lord of the Rings* is essentially about the very things these soldiers experience: friendship, sacrifice, loyalty to a cause higher than oneself, and, above all, the brutal reality of death. Army Chaplain R. J. Gore used *The Lord of the Rings* extensively during his tour of duty in Iraq, both in his sermons and on his weblog. During a prayer breakfast for the 84th Combat Engineers, he confessed that he had read the book multiple times since arriving in the theater. In a sermon he delivered on October 17, 2004, he formed an explicit connection between the book and its characters and the men and women in his care:

> Many of you have seen *The Lord of the Rings* movies, or read the books. Perhaps you feel a bit like Frodo when he found out that the Ring he received from his uncle, Bilbo, was the Ring of Power that was being sought once again by the Dark Lord himself. "I wish it need not have happened in my time," said Frodo. "So do I," said Gandalf, "and so do all who live to see such times. But that is not for them to decide. All we have to decide is what to do with the time that is given us."[4]

Gore goes on to acknowledge the enormous sacrifice required of the men and women in the field, the spiritual as well as the physical demands they face, and the temptation to despair and inaction. Frodo, Gandalf, and the others face "authentic struggles that parallel many of the struggles that you have experienced."

Clearly, soldiers identify with the struggles of Frodo and Sam and see in the hobbits' travails and hardships something of their own. *The Lord of the Rings* is thus a balm for many things, including deprivation and sacrifice. But if we accept Tolkien's own assertion that *The Lord of the Rings* is ultimately about Death and Immortality, the soldiers' affinity for the book becomes all the more meaningful and poignant.[5] For characters and readers alike, death is the real and continuous possibility that must be confronted.

Of course, soldiers are not the only ones who face the reality of death, and so the power of Tolkien's work is not limited to the theaters of war. Across the globe, battles of other kinds are fought: against disease, tyranny, or despair. In confrontations with death, both real and metaphorical, individual readers turn to *The Lord of the Rings* for comfort and reassurance. And so they should. For Tolkien, the central importance of any work lay not solely in its value as an aesthetic object but also in its "applicability to the thought and experience of readers."[6] A good book, in this view, is one to which readers turn when they come to pivotal moments in their own lives. What matters about a story is how people *use* it. Stories are "proverbs writ large" that function as a framework for dealing with those "typical, recurrent situations" that arise in everyday life, death and loss among them.[7]

Currently, forensic scientists classify death in one of six ways: homicide, suicide, accident, natural, iatrogenic, and indeterminate.[8] But these objective classifications do not answer an innate human need to make death *mean* something. Falling in battle defending one's country and being caught in the crossfire of a gang war are perceived as two totally different deaths, even though they both fall under the category of "homicide"—death caused by another individual's action) and may even involve precisely the same means, penetration of the body by a bullet. But one is heroic, the other tragic. What differs between the two is not the method but the message: we, as modern people, have inherited a tradition that insists that the *way* an individual dies matters. The media is full of references to "heroes who sacrificed themselves for freedom" and "the tragic deaths" of murder victims. Without even being aware of it, we rehearse, again and again, medieval conceptions of "good" and "bad" deaths.

In a sense, then, *The Lord of the Rings* works like an *ars moriendi*—a guide to the art of dying well. But it goes beyond that. Many modern views about the nature of death and dying are rooted in the Middle Ages that Tolkien studied and loved. These ideals continue to linger in what Raymond Williams calls the "residual" element of culture, which "has been effectively formed in the past, but . . . is still active in the cultural process, not only and often not at all as an element of the past, but as an effective element of the present."[9] Three great themes of death that pervade contemporary and medieval culture are united in *The Lord of the Rings:* the way we die, the need to remember the dead, and, above all, the lingering apprehension of what lies beyond the grave. Like our medieval ancestors, we still talk about what it means to die as a hero, a traitor, or a coward; we still make decisions about ways to honor and acknowledge the departed; we still seek to appease and contain the dead. All these suggest a latent resonance between medieval and modern cultures and raise an issue not generally discussed in contemporary society but present nonetheless: our deeply rooted belief that *how* one dies matters. The ways the peoples of Middle-earth face the prospect of their own deaths reveals great deal about their morality, their worldviews, and their values—much as it does in our own. Thus, this book examines how *The Lord of the Rings* makes visible medieval concerns about death and dying that remain applicable (but largely unnoticed) in modern society.

It is not my purpose to argue, as William Blisset did, that *The Lord of the Rings* is "the last literary masterpiece of the Middle Ages."[10] For all his longing for the Middle Ages, Tolkien lived and wrote in the twentieth century and was subject to its pressures and interpretations. Nevertheless, Tolkien was a medievalist, and many of his ideals are rooted in the Old Norse, Old English, and Middle English sources he studied, taught, and loved. My purpose is to explore those elements and show how *The Lord of the Rings* makes visible those residual, specifically medieval, concerns about death and the nature of dying that have been often overlooked. The first chapter, "The Wages of Heroism" focuses on those characters whose deaths represent medieval (and modern) ideas about "good" deaths. The death of Théoden King, for instance, neatly enfolds both medieval and modern conceptions of the "heroic death," while Gandalf's self-sacrifice in the Halls of Moria follows the example of Christ and therefore represents the highest of Christian ideals. Boromir and Aragorn, too, are given noble ends. Working in parallel, the second chapter, "The Bitter End," will focus on the meaning and significance of the "bad" deaths in *The Lord of the Rings,* specifically those of Gollum, Denethor, Saruman, and Gríma Wormtongue. Painful as these deaths may be to witness, they also demonstrate the importance of free will: as in many depictions in medieval literature, each of these characters are given multiple opportunities to turn away, and yet they do not. By presenting both "good" and "bad" deaths, Tolkien reminds us that it is not death itself that has the final say but the way we choose to face it.

The very fact of death necessitates some form of commemoration, which Tolkien presents in both the physical structure of monuments and tombs and the less concrete form of song and story. Chapter 3, "Songs and Stones," examines the ways the dead are simultaneously present and absent. The Dwarves, for instance, associate the dead with permanence; they believe that they are made from stone and so in stone they are buried. The Rohirrim, an essentially verbal and agrarian society, sings frequently of the heroes of their past; they are comfortable with their dead and live side by side with them. The people of Gondor, however, build elaborate monuments that are nevertheless hidden away and unvisited. In all cases, though, the dead are constantly present, and Tolkien's examination of the death practices of his various created cultures and races acknowledges the benefits of memory as well as the price of denying the dead.

Not all the dead, however, lie quietly in their graves. The fourth chapter, "Haunting the Dead," details the three separate ghost stories that appear in *The Lord of the Rings*. Frodo's encounter with the barrow-wight, for instance, clearly parallels Old Norse stories of the *draugar;* later, the crossing of the Dead Marshes inevitably recalls medieval stories of corpse candles. And finally, Aragorn's summoning of the Grey Company is redolent with images drawn from medieval accounts of the Wild Hunt. Each of these events incorporates medieval traditions and folklore, but Tolkien uses them to reinforce his unstated, and perhaps even unconscious, ideas about the benevolent meaning of death. For all their disparity, Tolkien's ghost stories are united by a common theme: they each emphasize not the injustice of death but the injustice of not being allowed to die.

Finally, in "Hope without Guarantees," the book returns to Tolkien's idea of applicability, examining how ordinary people apply each of the three themes. The ideas of "good" and "bad" death, for instance, are still very much at play. The dead still require commemoration, and some people, as we see in Staff Sergeant Holcomb's memorial, use Tolkien's story to do it. Inspired by Tolkien, they write their own Middle-earth tales to deal with grief and use passages from *The Lord of the Rings* on their own gravestones. We are no less haunted by the presence of the dead than our ancestors were, but Tolkien helps ease our misgivings about the uncertainty of death.

And underneath and behind it all lies the ultimate message of *The Lord of the Rings:* hope without guarantees.

Obviously, such an undertaking will leave out much that should be said, beginning with Tolkien's encounters with death throughout the entirety of the Silmarillion. Throughout the entire legendarium, several major characters die, including Thorin, Fĕanor, Finrod Felagund, Fingolfin, Morwen, Beren, and Lúthien Tinúviel. All of these are interesting portrayals in their own right and represent important aspects of Tolkien's cosmology. But because of the popularity of *The Lord of the Rings,* and because it was completed more or less to Tolkien's satisfaction (as the rest of the legendarium was not), I have chosen that text as the most likely place to start.

CHAPTER I

The Wages of Heroism

The Lord of the Rings is a book filled with death. More than fifty named characters die within its pages, nine of them major characters. In addition, there are songs and ballads that commemorate events long past, ruins and monuments that link the living to the dead, tales of ghosts and restless dead that haunt borderlands, and thousands of nameless individuals who fall during the long struggle against Sauron. None of these people ever existed, of course, and yet we cannot help but believe their deaths somehow matter—not because they themselves lived but because we recognize in their experiences something of our own. For the characters and the readers of *The Lord of the Rings*, death goes far beyond the inevitable sense of loss that accompanies it; it is a real and continual possibility lying at the end of all their actions. In the book as in the Primary World, death is the inevitable outcome that each individual must face, the fear that must be overcome. Its presence, spoken and unspoken, fills almost every page. Tolkien certainly didn't intend it that way, and yet when he re-read the book he realized that "the real theme" of *The Lord of the Rings* was "Death and Immortality."[1] Much has been written about Tolkien's philosophy of immortality and the Gift of Death. Much more remains to be said about the way those nine major characters die, and still more about the consequences of those deaths for those who remain behind. The ways the peoples of Middle-earth face death and respond to the dying reveal a great deal about their morality, their worldviews, and their values—much as they do in our own.

Though Plato was perhaps the first to acknowledge that the very act of living is but preparing for death, and the Bible reminds us seven times that Heaven and earth will pass away, these observations seem far too general to be of much help when facing one's own mortality.[2] In the Middle Ages, however, people responded to the uncertainties of life by writing conduct books for everything from "hunting and hawking . . . [to] table manners for children,"—which extended right into guidebooks for dying a proper death.[3] These books, the *ars moriendi,* or "art of dying," first appeared around the middle of the fifteenth century and remained international bestsellers until the beginning of the eighteenth.[4] Caxton's abbreviated version, somewhat lavishly titled "Here begynneth a lytill treatise shorte and abreged spekynge of the arte and craft to knowe well to dye" (1490), apparently translated by Caxton, was among the first books to come off the English printing press. At least five more English variations of the *ars moriendi* were published within the next fifteen years.

Although the traditional *ars moriendi* no longer exist as such, literature occupies a unique place in our understanding of death. For one thing, all texts belong to our collective experience; once published, a book is theoretically available to everyone. And for another, it can provide us with examples we are unlikely to face in any individual life but that can enhance our experience of life and death in significant ways. It is worth noting that when discussing attitudes toward death, historians, sociologists, anthropologists, physicians, and even archaeologists turn to *literary* sources to discover what people of a given time were thinking and feeling about death. Wills and testaments can reflect burial practices and funerary rites; chronicles give us dates, places and names; monuments mark changing attitudes toward the fate of the soul and body. But literature puts words in the mouths of the dying and gives them the chance to speak. The experience of others, even fictional others, teaches us about the myriad ways of facing death, whether with dignity and courage or fear and despair, and in so doing provides us with blueprints for the ways we might face our own deaths when the time inevitably comes. *The Lord of the Rings* is an important text because it provides its readers multiple models for their own moments of passing.

Today, the dying are usually relegated to hospitals or nursing homes, removed from society, although recent trends toward hospice care have started to influence popular perceptions.[5] A recent article in the *Atlantic* pointed out that Americans in particular have problems facing the inevitability of death, although the phenomenon is by no means limited to the United States.[6] Death takes place offstage, as it were, and so the manner of dying becomes less influential—at least, on the surface. But the traditions of ages are not so easily set aside. Only in modern times has death been separated from everyday experience, and even so the idea that a person's deeds in life have a consequence in death has not disappeared. Even today, when a good person dies, people console themselves by saying, "She's surely resting in the arms of God." In the case of less desirable individuals, however, the phrase becomes "He'll get what's coming to him." In the first case, death is seen as a reward; in the second, it becomes the hope for retribution. Without even being aware of it, we rehearse medieval conceptions of "good" and "bad" deaths: "The moral significance of one's life was thought to be complemented by the specific kind of death one met: whether it was peaceful and expected, or sudden and violent. Thus the precise manner of one's death, as much as the moral quality of one's life, had bearing upon one's fate in the afterlife."[7] In a variety of cultures and historical periods, one's behavior in life determined one's fate in death. In the Middle Ages, perceptions of "good" and "bad" death were heavily influenced by societal ideals of the heroic death as well as the traditions of the *ars moriendi*. Thus, the ideals of the *ars moriendi* and the literary portrayals of the heroic death not only provided guidelines for the way to die, they promoted the way to live. Furthermore, they reinforce important cultural norms of "right" and "wrong": the prospect of a punishment that endures even into the afterlife provides, in theory at least, a good reason for behaving well in this one.

In principle, the details of the *ars moriendi* were comparatively simple. First, the dying individual, often given the generic name Moriens, is advised to prepare constantly for death, since no one knows when or how it will come about. Second, he or she is warned about the five temptations—failure of faith, desperation (despair), impatience, vainglory, and unwillingness to let go of worldly things—and asked to refute them. Third are the interrogations, a series of questions designed to reinforce and affirm the values of the Church. Fourth is the *imitatio Christi*, where Moriens is encouraged to focus on Christ's actions on the cross as a guide. At this point, the attention switches largely to those surrounding the dying; they are first given a series of prayers to say for the benefit of the departed and then given an outline for the proper care and preparation of the body. Because clergy wrote the various tracts of the *ars moriendi,* the vast majority of the text is concerned with the religious aspects of dying, filled with prayers, orisons, and saintly quotations. But nestled among all the ritualized clerical trappings of death are glimpses of everyday human concerns—the need to dispose of worldly possessions, for instance, or the deep reluctance of the dying soul to part with the people he or she has loved on earth. The books outlining how to go about dying properly were wildly popular, best sellers in their day.[8]

The guidelines governing the proper way to face death, then, extended past the moment of death and into the realm of everyday life. So deeply are these ideas embedded in our social psyche that they often remain "unpacked and literally abstract in our presentations of them"—but they remain nonetheless.[9] From *Beowulf* to *Star Trek,* Western society has internalized what it means to die a good death, and most people intuitively know what a good heroic death should look like.

These, then, are the conventions surrounding literary heroic deaths. In poems such as *Beowulf* and *The Battle of Maldon,* the precise traits of a heroic death are clearly outlined. First, the hero delivers a heroic speech, wherein he—and it is usually a "he," though there are exceptions—acknowledges the likeliness of his eventual death in the looming battle, but pronounces that he must go anyway, because it is his duty or because it will ensure that his deeds will be remembered, or sometimes both. Traditionally, a heroic death presupposes death in battle; moreover, it is usually a battle that seems unwinnable, against an otherworldly monster or almost insurmountable odds. Once the battle begins, the hero can neither retreat nor surrender, however wounded he may be: to do so would bring down death and destruction on his own head and ensure a dreadful fate for those under his protection. Sometimes, he may withdraw for a short time, to rest and recover slightly from his wounds, but always he must return to the battle. He cannot relent until his enemy is slain. But the hero has been mortally wounded in the process, and frequently his weapon is destroyed or ineffective. His companions rush forward to aid him, but it is too late. The hero can do no more. And so, even as his enemy is destroyed, he brings about his own death. Before he dies, though, he expresses some hope that he will pass into the next world, shares his last wishes, and expresses his affection for those he leaves behind. And so he dies on the field of battle among the detritus of his victory and the grief of his friends. It is a good death.

Of all the deaths presented in *The Lord of the Rings,* that of Théoden King most overtly follows this pattern. When he rides to the Battle of Pelennor Fields, he knows it will likely be his last. Indeed, he hardly expected to survive the previous one. He has already endured great hardship: he has outlived his only son, defeated the forces of Isengard, and overcome the temptation to yield to the voice of Saruman. And now he proposes to ride to the aid of Gondor, where he will face an enemy no less indomitable than the Dark Lord himself—or at least the vast army the Dark Lord has gathered. He knows that if they fail, it really will be the war to end all wars: if Sauron wins, his people will endure nothing but misery and thralldom, as long as the world endures.

So Théoden King rides to war, one last time. Like his prototype, Beowulf, he recognizes that it is his right and duty to lead his people, to defend them with his last breath if need be. He does not actively seek death, but neither does he fear it. If he must die, better to do it among his warriors, where he can put his experience to use and protect his people as long as he can. When his nephew Éomer urges him to stay behind in the relative safety of Harrowdale, Théoden replies that doing so will accomplish nothing and that his death in battle would bring no grief. So it is really no surprise that when Hirgon arrives with the Red Arrow, representing Denethor's urgent request that the Rohirrim come to Gondor, Théoden replies that he will lead his forces to the fight, though he does not really expect to return (*RK,* V, iii, 775).

That the Red Arrow is an object of profound significance seems obvious, both from the fact that Denethor has sent it with no other real message and from Théoden's reaction to it. It is a tangible reminder of the ancient bond between Rohan and Gondor, an alliance that has stood for 508 years, where each promised to come to the aid of the other. When he sees it, Théoden knows for certain that the outlook is bleak indeed. He could refuse. The Rohirrim have just faced down an enemy of their own, leaving their army weakened and their people battered. But once Gandalf frees him from the manipulations of Gríma Wormtongue, Théoden has shown himself to be a good and wise king. It was his intention to ride to the aid of Gondor all along, but now he knows his aid is needed. "Old friendship and oaths long spoken" is motivation enough. "Even if Rohan itself felt no peril, still we would come," he tells Hirgon (*RK,* V, iii, 782). It hardly matters if the "old friendship" Hirgon speaks of lies between Denethor and Théoden, or even if they knew each other at all. Nor is it important if the "oaths long spoken" refers to the original bonds between Cirion and Eorl or renewed oaths spoken at the ascension of each new steward and king: Théoden's people have made a promise, and they will keep it.

Thus, Théoden's motives are honorable and above reproach, even for cynical modern readers. Modern audiences tend to be suspicious of someone who does a good deed with the aim of winning praise or fame (*lof*), although these ends were exactly what motivated an Anglo-Saxon warrior in the first place. Keeping a promise, however, still matters to most people. In this way, Tolkien smooths over the rough edges Anglo-Saxon and Gothic motivations that inspired the character, even as he allows those same motivations to remain out in the open.[10] Four times, the word "glory," a common translation of *lof,* is used in association with the death of Théoden King: three times during the Battle of Pelennor Fields and once during his funeral song. "Doom," the modern equivalent of *dom,* also appears in that song, although there it carries its modern meaning of "fate, destiny" instead of its Anglo-Saxon connotation of "judgement" or "fame." For an Anglo-Saxon warrior, the praise of one's contemporaries was the only way of ensuring immortality. The last word in *Beowulf,* the most famous of the Anglo-Saxon poems, is *lofgeornost,* "most eager for fame," which suggests that Beowulf was not motivated by greed or power, but the "reputation and renown" that alone could ensure that his name would live on after his death.[11] The speaker in the poem we call *The Seafarer* states quite bluntly:

> Forþon bið eorla gehwam æftercweþendra
> lof lifgendra lastworda betst
> *Seafarer,* ll. 72–73

[Therefore for all men the praise of those who speak of him afterward, the [ones still] living, is the best memorial]

This kind of glory—the hope that his deeds will be remembered—is the best Théoden hopes for *for himself.* He has not given up hope entirely.

Though he recognizes that he rides to the greatest battle of his age, "in which many things shall pass away," *many things* is not *all things* (*RK*, V, iii, 786). It is an important difference, as the example of Denethor will demonstrate (see chapter 2). Hoping that one's deeds will be remarkable enough to tip the scale in a battle that cannot honorably be avoided is not the same as seeking out fame for fame's sake. Théoden knows even before leaving Rohan that he and his Riders will be badly outnumbered, although just how badly will not become clear until they reach Pelennor Fields. Even after receiving the Red Arrow, he continues to make provision for the future of his people, protecting them as best he can regardless of his own fate. He does not take Éomer's advice to remain behind in Edoras but leads his troops into battle. As Janet Brennan Croft notes, "the heart of the morality of leadership, for Tolkien, was the willingness of a leader to take the same risks as those he leads," and Théoden certainly meets and even surpasses that expectation.[12] Not only does he join the fighting outside Minas Tirith, he puts himself in the center, where the fighting will be heaviest. Refusing to be daunted by the sheer weight of numbers or the horrible smell of death, he calls his men to battle in a clear voice and springs into action, riding faster even than the knights of his own *éored* (*RK*, V, v, 819). It is a stirring moment, as the King of Rohan leads his men, his golden shield flashing, his white horse shining, the fresh wind carrying promise of victory at the turning of the tide. Though an old man, he leads the charge against the chief of the Haradrim and singlehandedly brings down both standard and bearer: a clear token of victory. In many tales, such a moment would be the king's finest hour, and he would ride triumphantly homeward.

But not here. Théoden is pitted against a foe greater than he knows. From across the field, the Nazgûl senses the change in the weather and comes to confront the old man, scattering the King's *éored* or causing the horses to cast their riders from their saddles from sheer terror. The isolation of the hero, too, "has a long history in heroic literature, not least in the heroic legends of Scandinavia."[13] Théoden alone remains in the saddle, undaunted even by the Lord of the Nazgûl. Then a dart pierces Snowmane's side, causing the horse to fall and crush his rider beneath him. It is not Théoden's fate to destroy the Nazgûl, but there is no need: he has already done all a hero needs to do. His courage and military prowess bring

Éowyn to the precise place she needs to be in order to face the Lord of the Nazgûl; her love for the old man (and, in turn, Merry's love for her) gives her the courage to bring the Witchking down.

True to ancient tradition, Tolkien gives the King of the Mark a last chance to speak, and when he does, his words are filled with grace and acceptance. He at once forgives Merry for disobeying his orders, recognizing the hobbit's courage instead of chastising his insubordination. Instead of lamenting his death, the King focuses on what good he has accomplished: "I go to my fathers. And even in their mighty company I shall not now be ashamed" (*RK*, VI, vi, 824). Although Karen Rockow has observed the ambiguity of this phrase—it might refer either to a belief in the afterlife or merely to Théoden's own resting place among the barrows of his ancestors—the King's words reveal his belief that he has done something significant and worthy.[14] He has lead his people through two battles against impossible odds, leading the final charge himself in both cases, and, in his final battle, destroyed the standard of the black serpent and retained his courage even before the Lord of the Nazgûl himself. No small accomplishment, that. And so he lies, slowly dying from the wounds sustained by being crushed by his horse. The internal bleeding, broken bones, and ruptured organs would make it difficult for him to speak, and thus Théoden's last words are few but poignant. With his dying breath, he hails his nephew as the new King of the Mark, wishes him victory, and sends his love to Éowyn. And then he dies, having served his people well and honorably and with his warriors gathered around him (*RK*, VI, vi, 825). In his own eyes and in the eyes of his people, he has died with courage and dignity, and it is enough.

Théoden King thus embodies the ideal death of the Germanic hero, at least as closely as we understand it from surviving poetry. Whether or not such an ideal ever really existed is another matter entirely. One possible example is the famous story of Cynewulf and Cyneheard, appearing in the Parker version of the *Anglo-Saxon Chronicle*—if the reader is willing to ignore that the whole episode begins with Cyneheard's decision to rebel against King Cynewulf in the first place.[15] Another famous example is the encomiastic *Waldere*, written as propaganda for Walter of Aquitaine, and, most famous of all, the inspiring *Battle of Maldon*, likely commissioned by Earl Byrthnoth's daughter to make his defeat sound rather more like a victory.[16] The poems recalled what a hero *should* be, not necessarily what a warrior actually *was.*

Something of this idealism might be owed to the new religion: Christianity. After all, every poem and story we have was written by Christians for Christians. But even so, those early scops and bards had to make the stories acceptable, interesting, and relevant to people. A society's values do not disappear overnight. Instead, it seems that the coming of Christianity merely absorbed and even "accommodated the ancient warrior code" into the new religion.[17] War for the sake of war slowly metamorphosed into the concept of war for the sake of peace. Old ideas about the life laid down with honor, courage, and loyalty became infused with new ideas about steadfastness, faithfulness, self-control, and sacrifice. It is precisely this characteristic—this putting one's own good behind the good of others—that makes this idea distinctly medieval. Greek and Roman heroes, like Achilleus and Heracles and even Odysseus, took to the field *for their own gain,* because it was their only means of assuring immortality. For Christians, that immortality is already assured, meaning that heroism gradually evolved to include the concepts of humility and sacrifice. Thus, *The Dream of the Rood* casts Christ as the young hero leaping onto the Cross to fulfill his duty; *Judith* tells of a young heroine who risks her life for her people; Byrthnoth dies a Christian death. Even Beowulf, sometimes castigated for his unseemly pride, nevertheless speaks of his need and duty to protect his people. *Frod folces weard,* he calls himself, "old guardian of the people." And while it is true that Beowulf says that the best a warrior can hope for is that people will speak well of him after he dies, as Achilleus might, it is hard to imagine Achilleus joking that if Grendel ate his head, at least Hroþgar would be spared the funeral expense.[18]

The world, then, had changed, and with it the concept of a hero. No longer was the gaining of *lof* or *dom* sufficient unto itself; a true hero, in the new understanding, would be someone who undertook his or her actions for the greater good: for God, for freedom, for justice. The result was, as Guy Bourquin puts it, a sort of "lexis of hero-hood" which defined a hero as "he who MANIFESTS himself TO others FOR THE SAKE of others."[19] This is, of course, as precise a definition of Gandalf the Grey as one could wish. Although the original readers of *The Lord of the Rings* had no way of knowing it, Gandalf is not a human wizard at all but another type of being entirely. The Tale of Years records only that the five Istari appear about a thousand years into the Third Age, sent to Middle-earth by the Valar to help Elves and Men resist the growing power of Sauron. Not until the publication of *The Silmarillion* in 1977 did it become clear that Gandalf (or, for that matter, Saruman or Sauron) is a Maia, a spiritual being only slightly less powerful than the Valar, present at the creation of the universe. As his true self, he had no physical form except when he chose to take it; he was more often experienced as "fair visions" or "the promptings of wisdom" by which he invisibly guided the Firstborn.[20] Nevertheless, when he did come to Middle-earth, he became incarnate, subject to all the limitations that having a body entails, including getting tired, hungry, and cold. By the end of the Third Age, Saruman had succumbed to the temptation of the Ring and Rhadagast too became limited; no one knows what happened to the Blue Wizards. In the end, then, only Gandalf remained true to that mission, even to the point of death.

To be sure, a wizard seems an unlikely candidate for a heroic death. For one thing, the simple status of "wizard" marginalizes characters, setting them at the boundaries of human society. If the wizard is evil, he or she is often the foil the hero must overcome; if the wizard is good, he or she will be the friend and counselor who guides the hero to victory. In either case, the wizard is not the hero.[21] Wizards seldom appear in battle, and when they do, their battles are magical rather than physical. Unless equipped with magical devices, ordinary men and women have no defense against a wizardly assault. That is exactly why wizards' battles were viewed as so fundamentally unheroic: it breaks the unspoken code that the hero had to have, every pun intended, a fighting chance. So it was that Old Norse society, for instance, thought "magic reprehensible not because it is violent but because it is unfair. One is supposed to kill enemies in honest combat, not through the furtive rituals of sorcery."[22] Second, wizards typically die—if they die at all—distinctly *un*heroic deaths. *Gísli Sursson's Saga*, for instance, records that the sorcerer Þorgrímr died by being stoned to death with a sack tied over his head, and his body was covered over with mud and stones.[23] The *Kalevala* features a strange sort of wizards' battle, in which the defeated man is sunk up to his neck in a swamp. Even Merlin, the greatest of medieval wizards, meets his end by being tricked into giving up his powers and being trapped in a tree. These are memorable deaths (or ends), but they are hardly the heady stuff of the death of Arthur or other medieval heroes.

And yet, Tolkien's Gandalf undoubtedly *is* a hero. True, he plays the traditional role of friend and counselor, but he is also capable of taking action at need. In fact, he acts very much like a typical Anglo-Saxon hero. It is he, for instance, who heads up the Fellowship as it leaves the temporary haven of Rivendell. He leads the company across the wasteland and saves it from freezing to death on the slopes of Caradhras. He challenges the Hound of Sauron (*FR*, II, iv, 290). By that point in the story, Gandalf has overcome trolls, goblins, wolves, and Wargs; escaped the clutches of Saruman; singlehandedly driven off five Nazgûl; and endured the darkness of Moria—alone. Aragorn may be the guide, but Gandalf is undoubtedly the leader.

For that reason, when push comes to shove, the Company will follow him even into the Mines of Moria. The very name means "black pit" or "black abyss," and even before we cross its doors, we are allowed to feel something of the dread it inspires. Of all the Company, only Gandalf and Aragorn have been inside, and they do not speak willingly of the experience. Boromir would rather pass through the domain of Saruman, whom he knows is a traitor capable of imprisoning Gandalf himself, than risk entering the Mines. Even the hobbits, who know almost nothing of the world beyond their borders, dread the name of Moria. And yet into Moria they go, driven by chance and cruel necessity. There, Gandalf guides them past the terror of the Watcher in the Water and the remains of the fallen Dwarves at the gates and up into the ruins of Dwarrowdelf. For a moment, we get a glimpse of what a great realm Moria must once have been—but only a glimpse. Soon thereafter, the company finds itself trapped in the Chamber of Records, the very place where the Dwarves made their last stand. It is an ominous sign, soon followed by even more ominous sounds: the drumming in the deep. Gandalf realizes at once what the sound means, yet he shows no fear. Although Boromir and Aragorn both spring into action, Gandalf quickly takes command. He orders that the east door be left open; he challenges the enemy and assesses how many there are. The orcs attack. A fight ensues. Frodo is injured. Gandalf orders the retreat. As the Company makes its escape, Gandalf stays behind to lay a spell of holding on the door so that the orcs cannot come after them. But while laying the spell, he suddenly faces another force, a being so powerful that Gandalf himself is shaken. The clash of the two forces proves to be too much for the door and it shatters, bringing down the wall and the roof with it (*FR*, II, v, 318–19).

What the wizard encountered, of course, is the Balrog, one of the few creatures in Middle-earth equal in power and might to Gandalf. The *Valaquenti* describes the Balrogs as "scourges of fire that in Middle-earth were called the Balrogs, demons of terror" (*Silm*, 31). Indeed, everything about the Balrog of Moria is replete with the imagery of Hell: shadow and fire define from it; flame and smoke surround it; power and terror precede it. It is, in Milton's famous phrase, "darkness visible;" perceived more than seen.[24] Its very form is obscure: the text says explicitly that it is *maybe* man-shaped and the shadows about it can take the shape of wings (*FR*, II, v, 321, 322). Natural light fades before it, and yet flame reaches up to greet it. In fact, the most tangible thing about it is its weaponry. Though a flaming sword would surely be sufficiently imposing in itself, the Balrog also wields a whip, further underscoring its infernal associations: medieval iconography often shows demons torturing their victims with whips. For instance, the Guthlac scroll, circa twelfth century (now held at the British Library), depicts the saint being whipped by a demon; a panel of glass in Chartres Cathedral (1193) shows St. Anthony being thrashed by demons with whips; Virgil and the pilgrim see spirits running from demons with whips in the first chasm of Dante's *Inferno* (1308).

No mortal can stand against such an enemy. Even Elves are dismayed by it, as Legolas's reaction makes clear. It is true that some Elves fought successfully against Balrogs in the distant past, but those were High Elves who had lived in the Light of Valinor. No one in the Company, not even Legolas, can claim such status. Gandalf alone has any hope of fighting a monster such as this, because he is of the same degree and kind as the Balrog, and perhaps even of the same spirit: they are both associated with power and flame. The difference lies not in their degree but in their purpose, Gandalf's to protect, the Balrog's to destroy. Gandalf reminds the Balrog of this fact when he warns: "I am a servant of the Secret Fire, wielder of the flame of Anor. You cannot pass. The dark fire will not avail you, flame of Udûn" (*FR*, II, v, 322).

Again, before the publication of *The Silmarillion,* readers had little hope of understanding precisely what Gandalf meant; "Secret Fire" and "flame of Udûn" seemed just more of the erudite language wizards use in their mysterious world of magic. But after its publication, and even more so with the subsequent publishing of the Histories of Middle-earth, it becomes clearer precisely what Gandalf is alluding to. In many places in these books, "Secret Fire" is another name for the "Flame Imperishable"—the source of all life, which resides with Ilúvatar.[25] Udûn, however, is the name of Melkor's first fortress, where he twisted many things from their original beauty into new forms that are horrible and corrupt (see *Silm,* 31, 50). I am not quite willing to state with Matthew Dickerson that the Battle on the Bridge represents the battle between heaven and hell, but certainly it is a contest between that which would save and that which would destroy, the fire that inspires and the fire that consumes.[26] In that sense, it is a microcosm of the larger battle.

And so at this point, Gandalf must make a terrible choice. For all he knows, the mission will fail without him. Because he is a Maia, he is the only member of the party who can stand up to Sauron—and to give Men and Elves aid in the resistance against Sauron was the point of his mission to Middle-earth in the first place. But then again, the Balrog is a Maia too, and so if Gandalf does not take immediate action, the quest could fail right then and there. It is a terrible choice: risk his life *now,* knowing that if he falls, the chances for the quest's success would be greatly diminished, or let the Company take on the Balrog, knowing that some of them would surely fail and die, but with some greater hope of success *later.* This part of the battle takes place entirely within Gandalf; the hobbits never see it, so the reader doesn't either. But it occurred, nevertheless. In a letter to Robert Murray, Tolkien explains:

> For in his condition it was for him a *sacrifice* to perish on the Bridge in defence of his companions, less perhaps than for a mortal Man or Hobbit, since he had a far greater inner power than they; but also more, since it was a humbling and abnegation of himself in conformity to "the Rules": for all he could know at that moment he was the *only* person who could direct the resistance to Sauron successfully, and all *his* mission was in vain.

He was handing over to the Authority that ordained the Rules, and giving up personal hope of success.[27]

Seen in this light, the battle between Gandalf and the Balrog takes on an entirely different dimension: it becomes a battle of conflicting choices between seemingly equal duties as well as a fight between wizard and demon, good and evil. The key word, however, is hope: giving up personal hope is not the same as giving up hope altogether. In fact, in this situation it is exactly the opposite: it requires that Gandalf puts his hope entirely into the hands of "the Authority" and then simply allows things to go as they will. Ordering his companions to run, Gandalf faces the Balrog alone. "You cannot pass," he says, and Tolkien, who has given the wizard so many emphatic passages in the scene immediately preceding this one, does not do so now. Having made his decision, Gandalf is calm, waiting—which only emphasizes the fear of the other characters watching events unfold. Then the sentence structure breaks into short, staccato passages, creating an intensifying rhythm that underscores intensity of the moment:

> From out of the shadow a red sword leaped flaming.
> Glamdring glittered white in answer.
> There was a ringing clash and a stab of white fire. The Balrog fell back and its sword flew up in molten fragments. The wizard swayed on the bridge, stepped back a pace, and then again stood still. (*FR,* II, v, 322)

Only now does Tolkien allow him to speak with passion: "You cannot pass!" he says a third time. And the Balrog responds in kind, leaping on the bridge, whirling its whip. Even as Aragorn and Boromir spring forward, running to Gandalf's aid, the wizard raises his staff and cracks the bridge, sending the Balrog plunging into the abyss. But even as it falls, the Balrog swings its whip again, and this time the thongs catch Gandalf around the knees, pulling him to the brink of the broken bridge. Even there, Gandalf's last thoughts are not for himself but for others: "'Fly, you fools!' he cried, and was gone" (322).

So the Fellowship witnesses Gandalf's last battle, replete with all the trappings of the conventional heroic death but enhanced by the distinctly sacrificial air and a profoundly personal connection to the hero. Théoden's death on the battlefield was glorious, and he died as he would have wished, for his ideals and his people. But Théoden's death was inevitable: he was mortal, doomed to die. Gandalf is not. He might have lived and continued in his mission for many years. Yet he chooses to sacrifice himself, taking the grave risk that Frodo and the rest can complete their missions without him. That he is a Maia does not ameliorate the pain of his decision; in fact, it becomes more intense, because he would not under ordinary circumstances be subject to death at all. But Tolkien makes it quite clear that Gandalf really does die: "these 'wizards' were incarnated in the life-forms of Middle-earth, and so suffered the pains both of mind and body. . . . Thus Gandalf faced and suffered death."[28] Like the mortals he serves, he suffers hunger, exhaustion, temptation, and sorrow; he is also capable of implacable determination, deep friendship, boundless joy, and great love. These qualities are all enhanced, not suppressed, by his dying; in fact, almost all are most visible at the moment of his death. His action has led a variety of authors to compare him to the ultimate Type in the Western world, that of Christ Himself: "Like Christ, Gandalf bore himself in humility, loyalty and the greatest love for all free peoples under the care of his labors."[29] But, as Richard Purtill so eloquently puts it, "Gandalf, who gives up his life for his friends on the bridge of Khazad-dûm, is not an allegorical mask for Christ: he is a free creature who freely answers the call to imitate Christ."[30] The example is perhaps a bit backward: since Tolkien deliberately placed the entire timetable of the legendarium in a pre-Christian world, the option of imitating the Messiah is unavailable. Tolkien certainly knew about Christ; Gandalf did not. Furthermore, Tolkien insisted that the "the Incarnation of God is an infinitely greater thing than anything I would dare to write."[31] Within the story, though, the manifestation of Gandalf the Grey reveals a willingness to sacrifice himself for the good of others: the highest form of heroism.

Théoden teaches us that "glory is not to be found in the hope of the hero, or in the hero's final victory, but rather in the hero's willingness to continue to fight the battle *even though he knows he is fated to die in the end.*"[32] Gandalf teaches us the life freely given for the sake of another is noble and valuable and that, moreover, we are free to make that choice. Bourquin's definition of the hero as one who becomes known to others for the sake of others could hardly be better represented. Gandalf the Grey must have been, on some level, sorely tempted to abandon the battle, believing as he did that he was the only one who could protect Frodo and see the Quest through to its end. But he resisted temptation, and although the text never says it, it somehow seems clear that the Quest would have been more likely to fail if he succumbed. Instead, Gandalf chose to stay and fight, placing his hope in the hands of a power greater than himself. He had to hope that things would come out all right without him. And by surrendering not to the Balrog but to hope, and dying, he won.

Of course, not everyone successfully overcomes temptation. Boromir of Gondor is perhaps most notable for the fact that he *doesn't* resist the temptation of the Ring. Like many of us, he falters. He fails, and ultimately, he falls. Though he appears as traditional a hero as one could wish, he is the one who betrays Frodo's trust and tries to wrest the Ring from Frodo's guardianship, and his actions directly result in the breaking of the Fellowship. As such, he seems unlikely to be eligible for a heroic death. Nevertheless, Tolkien presents his actions with pity instead of condemnation. He uses Boromir's death to demonstrate that even the most flawed among us can die with courage and dignity, if they repent of their actions and partake of the grace and forgiveness that has always awaited them.

Initially, however, Boromir appears very much the traditional medieval hero. His are the dominant traits of Anglo-Saxon and Old Norse heroes: physical strength, pride, and prowess. He is noble, brave, and courageous—and focused solely on what *he* might achieve. He is reminiscent of Beowulf, though the impetuous Beowulf in his youth; he is proud, eager to prove himself, somewhat brash, quick to boast and slow to listen. Like Beowulf in Heorot, he speaks proudly of the toils of his travels and the accomplishments of himself and his people. Boromir is also faintly reminiscent of the Icelandic hero Grettir, who is defined above all by his strength. But both Beowulf and Grettir come to offer help, while Boromir has come to *seek* help and advice, though he is so proud that even desperate need will not allow him to ask directly.[33] Humility, however, was not a dominant trait of medieval heroes; one often had to promote oneself shamelessly if one was going to succeed. And it must be admitted that Boromir's qualifications are remarkable: he is the son of Denethor, Steward of Gondor, and an accomplished military leader; he has successfully negotiated the difficult journey to Rivendell entirely on his own. He

does not hesitate at all about putting himself forward, frequently inter-
rupting other members of the council and even challenging the wisdom
of their decision to destroy the Ring. He greets the news that Aragorn
is the Heir of Elendil with outright doubt (*FR*, II, ii, 241). Clearly, he
cannot imagine that any hero, much less a king, could be so self-effacing.

Nevertheless, Boromir is not completely unrecognizable as a hero to a
modern audience. After he joins the Fellowship, he repeatedly shows himself a brave man and an experienced warrior. Pippin in particular finds him
truly admirable; when the Fellowship is trapped in a sudden snowstorm
on the knees of Caradhras, Boromir helps Aragorn clear a path to safety
and then returns to help rescue the hobbits. He takes Pippin first, and
the young hobbit marvels at the strength that allows Boromir to carve a
passage for those that follow even while carrying Pippin on his back (*FR*,
II, iii, 285–86). Again and again, Boromir acts valiantly and courageously,
saving the Fellowship from certain death, fighting wolves and orcs by Aragorn's side.

Yet it is Boromir who first succumbs to the Ring. As it did with his
father, Denethor, pride defeats him, pride and a desperate need to defend his people. Initially, his pride seems externalized and patriotic; he
is quick to assert that the wisdom and knowledge of the Númenoreans,
though failing elsewhere, has not completely deserted Gondor. "All know
in Gondor that [Isildur] went first to Minas Anor and dwelt a while
with his nephew Meneldil, instructing him, before he committed to him
the rule of the South Kingdom," he tells the council (*FR*, II, ii, 246).
For the sake of his people, he is willing to admit, albeit reluctantly, that
Gondor lacks the strength to resist Sauron alone, and he seems to accept
the council's judgement that the Ring must be destroyed—though not
without protesting that the Ring should be used against its maker (261).

But as the Fellowship travels further south—nearer to Gondor and Mordor—Boromir reverts to his earlier misconception that the Ring should be
used, not destroyed. At first, the indications that the Ring is gaining hold
are so subtle that they are easily mistaken for his earlier nationalism: after
being forced off Caradhras, he proposes taking the easiest route to Gondor, though Gandalf immediately points out that such a route would take
them too near Saruman's stronghold of Isengard and take too long to boot.
After Gandalf's restraining presence is removed, however, his purposes for

remaining with the Company become ever more doubtful, particularly after
Galadriel removes the veil from him in Lórien. He responds to her testing
with words that seem too emphatic to be entirely true: "It need not be said
that I refused to listen. The Men of Minas Tirith are true to their word"
(*FR*, II, vii, 349). If it need not be said, why say it? What he *does* refuse
to say—what he thought the Lady had offered him—is significant, but it
becomes apparent soon enough: the chance to take the Ring to Gondor
and so win lordship and dominion for himself.

Though Boromir, like Grettir or Beowulf, is fundamentally a good
man, he is easy prey for the Ring. Just as it does for them, pride brings
about his downfall. In *Grettir's Saga,* the eponymous hero is marred by his
inability to function within the norms of his society, and his "obsessional
feeling that he must be superior to everything, and must keep proving this
superiority" ultimately lead to his destruction, just as Boromir's sense that
he is entitled to be Gondor's leader interferes with his ability to function
within the Company.[34] Beowulf, for all his greatness, insists on facing the
dragon by himself, dismissing his followers and entering the barrow alone.
But these actions also highlight Beowulf's ineffectualness; as Martin Puhvel observes, "Wiglaf fights [the dragon] effectively and incapacitates it,
whereas the great Beowulf had been able to do little except arouse it."[35]
Though he has been warned repeatedly that the Ring corrupts and perverts
even the strongest of wills and the best of intentions, Boromir continues to
believe that somehow *he* will be exempt from its manipulations. After leaving the safety of Lothlórien, the Ring's grip grows firmer, and Boromir's
behavior grows increasingly erratic. As the Company paddles down the
river toward their ultimate destination—whether Mordor or Gondor has
not yet been decided—Boromir sits "muttering to himself, sometimes bit-
ing his nails, as if some restlessness or doubt consumed him" and Pippin,
who admires him so greatly, catches "a queer gleam in his eye, as he peered
forward gazing at Frodo" (*FR*, II, ix, 373). The nearer they get to Mordor,
the more the Ring seeks to take control.

And finally, it does. When the Company at last reaches a point where
the decision must be made, and the Ring taken either to Mordor or to
Gondor, the true extent of Boromir's possession becomes manifest. Frodo,
knowing he must go to Mordor but nevertheless fearing the consequences
of that decision, asks to be given time alone to think. But as he wanders,

Boromir follows and at last approaches him as he debates with himself about which course to take. Boromir, of course, argues that Frodo should go to Gondor, where he insists the Ring can be used for good ends. When Frodo refuses, Boromir's facade slips, revealing with dreadful finality all that had been preying on his mind. Though he speaks in his madness of "our cause," it is really the Ring he seeks, and its ability to grant him the power he craves: "If any mortals have a claim to the Ring, it is the men of Númenor, and not Halflings. It is not yours save by unhappy chance. It might have been mine. It should have been mine. Give it to me!" (*FR*, II, x, 390). Boromir's vision leaves out what the Company must achieve, and his syntax suddenly starts to sound like Gollum's. He wants the Ring for his own glory, seeing it only as a vehicle for winning *lof* and *dom*. His desire for fame and his belief in his own ability to resist the Ring's evil lead to his death. Unable to see beyond himself, he fails to realize the Ring's terrible power acting upon him, and his actions trigger the breaking of the Fellowship: catastrophic for the Company, certainly, but disastrous for Boromir personally. Seeking to take the Ring from Frodo ensures his own defeat, one way or the other: if he had succeeded, the Ring would have destroyed him as surely as it did the Ringwraiths (even assuming he managed to keep possession of it). More likely, though, the Ringwraiths would have come for him and taken back the Ring, and the War would have been over before it had even begun.

But after Frodo escapes, Boromir recognizes his mistake: "What have I done? . . . A madness took me" (*FR*, II, x, 390). There is a strange ambivalence here, as even now Boromir reels between accepting the blame (What have *I* done?) and seeking to lay it elsewhere (*madness* made me do it). A crucial step in true repentance lies in accepting that one has done something wrong, taking personal responsibility, and then trying to correct it. Boromir is not quite there yet, but he is making progress. Still, he is not ready to make full confession. When he returns to the others, he admits that he has seen Frodo, that he tried to persuade the hobbit to go to Minas Tirith, and that he grew angry, even that Frodo put on the Ring—but does not reveal that Frodo donned the Ring as a consequence of his anger. "I grew angry and he left me," he says, followed by "He vanished"—as if the two events merely followed each other, not as if one were a consequence of the other—though the other members of the Company seem to have little enough trouble making the connection (*FR*, II, x, 395). Even when Aragorn prods him, Boromir will say no more. He is not yet ready to confess and make right his wrong. It may even be that he does not yet fully comprehend how very wrong he was—he bowed his head *as if* in grief, the narrator says, leaving room for that last small niggling worm of misgiving. There is little doubt that, operating under his own power, Boromir's guilt is real enough—but is it guilt that he failed his people, or guilt that he tried to take the Ring in the first place? If the Ring returned to Boromir's presence, would he be driven to sin again?

These are questions we cannot answer, because Tolkien did not write it that way. Instead, Aragorn gives Boromir a focused task: go and protect Merry and Pippin. Given the circumstances, it is a logical enough assignment and one that Boromir is eminently qualified to complete. But, unknowingly, Aragorn has also given Boromir a kind of penance, a task meant to allow an individual to atone for a particularly harmful deed. From at least the Fourth Lateran Council (1215) onward, part of the emphasis on penance has insisted that the penance be appropriate to the sin. Since Aragorn is not certain what has happened, he offers Boromir what R. W. Hanning calls "prudential penance," undertaken when "more than one solution is possible, and one cannot be absolutely certain that one's answer is the correct one."[36]

But for Boromir, Aragorn's answer does seem correct. We are not given the battle scene for another three chapters, and then it is very brief: only a paragraph of the fight described through Pippin's admiring eyes (*TT*, III, iii, 434). Certainly Boromir fought, and fought hard, pitching himself into the battle against the overwhelming odds required of the heroic death. But there is another element here, too, beyond the traditional heroic death of Théoden or the sacrificial heroic death of Gandalf: the air of atonement, of trying to make up for a bad deed. Whether or not his grief at the campsite was real, Boromir certainly seems to hold back nothing for himself now, not even a chance for his own survival. The process of redemption initiated by Aragorn now finds its completion in Boromir. True penance involves, among other things, "the sacrifice one makes for the sake of others," and in his battle to save Merry and Pippin, he atones for his attempt to subvert Frodo.[37]

The one step of the process that is missing, of course, is confession: Boromir has as yet told no one what he has done. According to medieval belief, as well as that of some modern Catholics, dying with a sin uncon-

fessed and unshriven means that the soul will go to Hell. Even the idealized
death of the *ars moriendi,* which was probably always more a literary and li-
turgical ideal rather than lived experience, allows room for final confession.
Tolkien gives Boromir this final chance. Sometime after the fight, Aragorn
finds Boromir slumped against a tree, pierced with many arrows, his broken
sword at his side. At last, Boromir confesses what he has done: "'I tried to
take the Ring from Frodo,' he said. 'I am sorry. I have paid.'" Clearly, Boromir sees his death at the hands of the brutal Uruk-hai as just repayment
for his attempt to take the Ring, just as his attempt to save the two younger
hobbits is his penance. And, though he remembers his responsibility to
Aragorn and the Company, his final thoughts are still for his people in
Gondor, fighting their own fight against Sauron. With his last breath, he
bids Aragorn to go to Minas Tirith and save them. While Aragorn does
not precisely promise that he will do so, he does console Boromir: "Be at
peace! Minas Tirith shall not fall!" And with a smile, Boromir dies (*TT,*
III, i, 404).

In the death of Boromir of Gondor, the conventions of Anglo-Saxon
and Old Norse heroic ideals and the *ars moriendi* meet and merge. Like
Théoden, Boromir dies a heroic death, but while Théoden's passing is
marked by a sense of greatness, Boromir's is pervaded by a sense of regret.
Like Beowulf, Boromir dies with a single individual at his side, a very
distant kinsman to whom he confesses his last sin and from whom he
receives absolution. He is surrounded by the trappings of a warrior—his
fallen enemies and his broken sword and cloven horn—but in other ways
he dies the death prescribed by the *ars moriendi.* His repentance, last-
minute though it is, falls within medieval convention, although the usual
order is reversed. Usually, an individual would commend all those dear to
him or her to God and then make final confession; Boromir makes his
last confession and then commends the care of his people to Aragorn.[38]
In this sense, he has "made a full confession to Aragorn, and wept as he
repented his actions: this is as near as a pre-christian [*sic*] man of virtue
can get to a Good Christian death."[39] Tragic though his death may be, it is
also redemptive; he has overcome his own pride, sacrificed himself for the
sake of others, and so died.

But his catastrophic actions also become catalytic: they give Frodo the
impetus to undertake the journey to Mordor; put Pippin and Merry on

the path to Fangorn; and cause Aragorn, Gimli and Legolas to pursue
the captured pair to Rohan, thus meeting the resurrected Gandalf and
coming to Théoden's aid in the nick of time. Boromir's death is, for all
involved, a *eucatastrophe,* a term Tolkien coined to denote "the sudden
joyous 'turn' that comes when a tragic event is suddenly seen to have had
unexpectedly fortunate consequences."[40] The forgiveness and grace that
mark Boromir's end form a distinct break from the militant heroic tradition, bringing the dying man, warrior though he is, closer to the conventions of the *ars moriendi.*

Only one individual in *The Lord of the Rings* follows the conventions of
the *ars moriendi* exactly, and, strictly speaking, he does not die within the
pages of the story itself. Though his death takes less than two pages to
describe, the passing of Aragorn is one of the most deeply moving scenes
in the story. Although he is undoubtedly one of the principal heroes of
The Lord of the Rings, Aragorn does not die the traditional heroic death
on the battlefield. Instead, he dies in his own city, his wife at his side, at
more or less a time of his own choosing—an event rarely seen in either the
Icelandic sagas or in the English texts, either Anglo-Saxon or post-Nor-
man. For all Aragorn's past heroism, his death follows the step-by-step
process outlined by the *ars moriendi*—the acceptance of death, the refusal
of temptation, the dispensation of worldly goods and the last farewell to
the family, and the final affirmation of faith.

Because Aragorn is of pure Númenorean descent, he is allowed to choose
the moment of his own death (though he may not, as we shall see, commit suicide). Having long since come to terms with his own mortality and
having accomplished all that was given for him to accomplish, he at last
feels his death coming on. He has lived long and well, and when he recognizes the signs of his impending death, he accepts them for what they are
and begins to prepare for the end. This step is the first prescribed by the
ars moriendi (and by the medieval church as a whole): to remember at all
times that one is going to die and to prepare for it accordingly.[41]

So Aragorn tells Arwen that the time has come: "My world is fading. . . .
[W]e have gathered, and we have spent, and now the time of payment
draws near" (*LR,* 1037). She immediately counters by asking him if he is
going to leave before his time, suggesting that really he might choose to
live just a little bit longer. Aragorn gently refuses this temptation, knowing

that if he does not willingly die now, he must die unwillingly later. Then he goes to the House of Kings wherein his ancestors lie, calls his son Eldarion to him, and gives him his crown and his scepter. Everyone leaves him except Arwen, who now functions as the religious attendant who allows the dying man to express his hope for the next world without mitigating the sorrow of leaving this one. Again she asks her husband to stay; for all her high knowledge and Elvish ancestry—or perhaps because of it—she could not understand, until this moment, the bitter finality of death. Aragorn, seeing her grief, does not demean her by offering false comfort. He has lost his mother, his friends, and countless others over the course of his long life, and knows the pain death brings to those who remain behind. Instead, he reminds her that they die in the hope of something greater beyond even Death: "In sorrow we must go, but not in despair. Behold! we are not bound for ever to the circles of the world, and beyond them is more than memory. Farewell!" (1038).

Aragorn's final statement echoes the sentiment typical of the *ars moriendi*, that a "goode deth ought better to be chosen than the euyl lyfe."[42] Though the rejection of the Ring of course refers to the actual refusal to accept the Ring's dominion in Middle-earth, it also serves a more subtle purpose: the Ring echoes "the circles of the world," and thus to die represents an escape from confinement and the promise of finding what Tolkien called "Joy beyond the circles of the world, poignant as grief."[43] But although he lives in a decidedly pre-Christian world, Aragorn's death focuses not on the accomplishments of this world but on the expectation of the next. Precisely because the Christian promise of Heaven is removed, Aragorn's death is the ultimate expression of hope.

These four examples of death fly in the face of Western tradition. Much of modern literature and culture teaches us that death is a failure of sorts: a failure of modern medicine to heal, a failure of soldiers to protect, even a failure of the terminally ill to endure. Tolkien's characters show us plainly that this is not so. In these instances, dying is not a case of failure or surrender but a victory. While none of these individuals particularly want to die, they accept it as a necessary risk if they are to remain true to their personal values: loyalty, freedom, honesty, hope, and love. Dying in defense of these things not a failure, but an expression of a life lived to the fullest. It is the affirmation that these virtues are so powerful, so important, that they insist on showing themselves even in (or perhaps especially) in an individual's last moments. This principle forms the heart of the medieval idea of the "good death," and it is no less valid now. Our battles are more likely to be fought against cancer than the Uruk-hai, but they still require courage; very few of us will try to steal a priceless object from a doomed hero, but many of us regret letting down a friend. Therefore, the lessons Théoden, Gandalf, Aragorn, and even Boromir teach are worth remembering when it comes time to face our own inevitable ends. Though Tolkien does face the possibility of other kinds of deaths, he reminds us that a good death remains equally possible, if we can only hope.

CHAPTER 2

The Bitter End

Although many of the deaths portrayed in *The Lord of the Rings* represent heroic ideals, a book so concerned with death could not avoid also depicting less than noble ends. Exactly what constitutes a "good" or "bad" death is subject to cultural interpretation, but in the Western world, two categories in particular have been viewed with deep suspicion: those violent against themselves (suicides) and those violent against others (thieves, traitors, and murderers). In the Middle Ages, the manner of one's death was held to reflect the moral quality of one's life, and that perception lingers even today.[1] For centuries, to be executed as a criminal has been judged "shameful by definition," while suicide was "considered a repugnant and criminal act" until the advent of modern psychology allowed a more humanist interpretation.[2]

In *The Lord of the Rings,* many of the "bad" deaths are in some way connected with the concept of treachery against basic human principles, the state, or the divine. It could be argued that Boromir's death is the result of his treachery, but his repentance and attempt at restitution absolve him from receiving the traitor's fate. Not so the others. Boromir's father, Denethor, betrays the responsibilities of leadership, resulting in the needless deaths of the soldiers under his command, and his final act is the ultimate expression of betrayal, against his people, his son, and himself. Gollum, whose entire life has been one of perpetual treachery, is betrayed by his own covetousness. The treason of Gríma Wormtongue and the apostasy of Saruman lead to the mutual destruction of both. But for all the horror and grief inspired by these deaths, each of them represents ways in which justice and order prevail over treachery and chaos.

If courage, love, penitence and faith can lead to good ends, then it stands to reason that despair, avarice, malice, impenitence, recalcitrance, and obduracy can lead to bad ones. Tolkien does not show these deaths out of pedantry, or even any kind of judgementalism, but as the necessary corollary to the good. Nor does he reject those who commit suicide in moments of anguish, as the examples of Nienor and Túrin make clear. What is not permissible is Denethor's cold, calculating decision to take his own life and the life of his son simply because he cannot have things his own way.

For this reason, of all the deaths in *The Lord of the Rings,* none typifies medieval reasoning about the "bad" death better than that of Denethor, Steward of Gondor. While classical civilization could tolerate and even glorify suicide, people in the Middle Ages thought it bad indeed. The very phrase "bad death" could even be used as a euphemism for suicide, and those who undertook such an act were often subject to legal and ecumenical action even after they had died. Suicide was an act of contempt for God because in so doing, one simultaneously thwarted the length God intended one's life to be and removed any possibility of His (or the Church's) forgiveness: one could not atone for the sin of self-murder or receive the Last Rites after one was already dead. Because suicide was regarded with such horror, people reasoned that any individual committing suicide must surely be under the influence of the Devil. After all, his specialty was, in a sense, leading people away from God. Therefore, suicide was a distinctly "*unspiritual* way of dying."[3] These apparently contradictory ideas about the cause of suicide—pride, despair, and even the Devil himself—represent part of the complex ways of thinking that embodied the Middle Ages and thus continue to inform our own.

Today, of course, people seldom blame the Devil when someone commits suicide, but it continues to be seen, probably correctly, as an act of despair. In an era in which the way of dying was every bit important as the fact of being dead, the ramifications could be horrible. A suicide risked not being buried in consecrated ground, or, worse yet, not being buried at all. In direct contradistinction to someone who had died a proper death, who would be honored by the entire community (consider Théoden, lying in state until Éomer could take him home), a suicide would be rejected by them all.

With the death of Denethor, Tolkien provides us a glimpse into the medieval way of thinking about suicide. In theory, Denethor's death should be grand and glorious: he is, after all, of Númenorean descent and holds the throne of Gondor in keeping for the King. He commands a powerful and diversified army. Yet it is Théoden who takes to the field, fighting and dying among his people. Denethor does exactly the opposite of what he should: instead of giving his life for his people, he takes it from them, committing suicide down among the dead, in a place where his people cannot follow. True, both he and Théoden have been subject to the manipulations of a corrupt Maia: Denethor falls to the misrepresentations of Sauron, Théoden to those of Saruman. True, Théoden had help—but so did Denethor, and from precisely the same source. Denethor's actions may even have led directly to the death of Théoden, preventing Gandalf from joining the battle at the critical moment (see *RK,* V, vii, 832).[4] The two men counterbalance each other, Théoden ascending while Denethor sinks. While the other great rulers of Middle-earth—Gandalf, Théoden, Aragorn, and Galadriel, for instance—all lead by example, Denethor prefers to supervise from behind, telling Pippin that a great lord such as himself "uses others as his weapons" rather than allowing himself to be used, even when he knows that the goal is just and honorable (*RK,* V, iv, 800; i, 741). He is too proud to live among those he leads and too stubborn to take good advice. His death, which could have been the grandest and most heroic in *The Lord of the Rings,* instead becomes a kind of anti–*ars moriendi,* a warning about the dangers of pride.

In one sense, Denethor's downfall begins well before the events of *The Lord of the Rings* unfold. Even in his youth, it is told, Denethor listened to counsel but then "followed his own mind" (*LR,* 1031). Like his elder son, Boromir, he trusts too much in his own abilities and too little in those of others, until ultimately he is willing to trust in no one and nothing but himself. This is *ofermod,* a troublesome word that Tolkien famously translated as "overmastering pride" and which inevitably has disastrous consequences for all involved.[5] In the medieval world, overmastering pride is foundation of sin, for *ofermod* led Satan to rebel against God and caused the death of Beorthnoth and his followers in *The Battle of Maldon. Genesis* B explicitly links Satan with *ofermod* in the moment of Satan's fall:

Ac he awende hit him to wyrsan þinge, ongan him winn up ahebban
wiþ þone hehstan heofnes waldend, þe siteð on þam halgan stole.

Deore wæs he drihtne urum; Ne mihte him bedyrned weorðan
þæt his engyl ongan   ofermod wesan (ll. 259–62)

[But he [Satan] turned himself into a terrible thing; he began to heave up
trouble against Him, against the high Ruler of Heaven, who sits on the
holy throne. Dear he was to our Lord, yet God might not be deluded that
his angel began to be overproud.]

The term *ofermod* is applied to Satan twice more before he is cast out of
heaven; because of his fall, sin and death come into the world.

On a far more human and forgivable scale, Beorthnoth's *ofermod* as recounted in *The Battle of Maldon* leads to his death as well as the deaths of
his most loyal followers.[6] In the midst of the battle, Beorthnoth snatched
defeat from the jaws of victory by allowing the Vikings to cross a causeway:

Ða se eorl ongan for his ofermode
alyfan landes to fela laþere ðeode (ll. 89–90)

[Then the earl in his overmastering pride began to yield too much of the
land to the hateful people]

Given the Vikings' superior numbers, Beorthnoth and his forces are soon
overwhelmed; Beorthnoth is the first to die. He may have made his decision to engage the Vikings for solid reasons, but the effect was disastrous
for those under his command.[7] Denethor follows the same pattern, allowing his excessive pride to lead him slowly but inexorably down the path
to destruction.

As is so often the case in human failings, Denethor begins with good
intentions. Though he possesses a keen intellect, he has never understood
the value of humility or the honor found in serving others (*RK*, V, i, 741).
He appears to adhere to long tradition and holds Gondor in keeping for the
King, but in reality, he covets that position for himself. Thus, in a sense,
his *ofermod* has led him to rebel against his rightful lord, which creates a

sort of double betrayal: to his duty as Steward on the one hand and to his own family on the other. He believes his younger son has become Gandalf's tool, and his favored older son has been killed in service to a cause Denethor regards as madness (iv, 795). And, in a final blow, the rightful King is on his way to the city, where he will, as Denethor sees it, supplant the line of stewards that have served Gondor for a thousand years.

All this has eaten away at Denethor's heart, but only in the moments just before his death is the extent of his despair made plain. When his city is besieged, he does not even appear to notice the plight of the ordinary soldiers fighting and dying below him. He, like Beorthnoth, suffers from "a failure to grow with one's responsibilities," and what might have been his finest hour becomes his final hour.[8] As Lord of Gondor, he is duty-bound to make some attempt to defend the city, but he betrays that responsibility. He withdraws instead into the tombs—a symbolic rejection of life if ever there was one—and prepares to immolate himself and Faramir, thereby setting off a dark, inverted mirror of the proper death outlined in the *ars moriendi*.

Though it is Théoden who says, "Dark have been my dreams of late," Denethor, too, has been plagued by dark thoughts (*TT,* III, vi, 504). His mind has been clouded with thoughts of death and defeat, but he has come to see death as an end in this world, not as preparation for the world to come, while resisting the Enemy is pointless. For Théoden, the opposite is true. Whereas Théoden sees his dying as a new beginning, an entry into the company of his ancestors, Denethor appears to see it as nothing more than an ending: an escape from this world, maybe, but not an entry into anything new. Suicide, especially when it is motivated by the conviction that death will come anyway, is the ultimate failure of faith, the first of the temptations refuted in the *ars moriendi*. When Gandalf, functioning in the clerical role, arrives in the houses of the Dead, his first act is not to surround Denethor with family and friends so that he can bless them and say farewell but to remove them from his presence so that he cannot harm them further. While he does not deny the possibility of Denethor's death, Gandalf tries to persuade the steward at least try to make that death count for something. But Denethor refuses, insisting that the battle against Darkness is hopeless (despair), so he and Faramir might as well give up and die side by side (complacence). Gandalf immediately counters that the time of his death is not his to choose (impatience); pointing out that killing himself in pride and despair, and taking his son with him to ease his own death (avarice) is a heathen act (*RK,* V, vii, 834, 835). In other words, Denethor has no right to kill himself when his people need him and no right at all to murder Faramir.

As others have pointed out, this confrontation between Gandalf and Denethor marks the only time in the entire story that Tolkien uses the word "heathen." The choice is significant. As a philologist, Tolkien was undoubtedly aware that, in the pre-Christian world, there was nothing particularly dishonorable about suicide. Since the world he created is likewise set before Christ, *all* the characters, even the most virtuous, are technically "heathen." And yet Tolkien, who so carefully struck out any other overt references to Christianity or to Christian belief, left this word in. Perhaps it simply reflects a certain historical accuracy carried over from the Primary World: the Germanic peoples did sometimes burn their dead on pyres, and some cultures do require that living family members immolate themselves with their burning family members.[9] Probably, though, the choice is more damning than that. Tolkien's own cosmology and his belief held that God always has and always will exist, whatever dates we mortals seek to impose on Him; He created all things and established the order of the universe. Presumably, then, the rules have not changed, even if our interpretation of them has. If this interpretation is correct, "heathen" in this context does not mean explicitly "not Christian" but something closer to "those who do not know or who do not acknowledge Eru or the Valar." Shippey points out that "the wise characters in *The Lord of the Rings* are often without hope and so near the edge of despair, but they do not succumb. That is left to Denethor, who will not fight to the last, but turns *like a heathen* to suicide and the sacrifice of his kin."[10] The difference is that while the others may lose hope for *themselves,* they never quite lose hope in something *greater* than themselves—the Valar or Eru or simply the power of a good story. In Tolkien's world, hope and humility go together. Denethor, who has lost all humility, likewise loses hope. And so, while characters like Théoden, for instance, can lead by example, putting themselves at risk, Denethor cannot bear to take that chance. The only opinion that counts to him is his own.

What Denethor cannot see—or will not permit himself to see—is that he is already a tool of other purposes. His pride, twisted by his grief over his wife's death, drives him to do what no other steward has dared to do: he looks into the *palantír,* trusting his own ability to resist the power of Sauron that controls it (*LR,* 1031). Though Denethor is too great to be completely mastered, Sauron slowly manages to poison his mind, turning his thoughts from the tasks he ought to do into bitter resentment toward what he cannot do. He yields not geographic territory but mental ground, thus surrendering his people to Sauron before the battle has even begun.

In the medieval tracts, this is precisely how Satan works: leading an individual to despair through a series of small missteps, until at last the victim sees no way out but taking his or her own life. Alexander Murray's study of suicide in the Middle Ages reveals that of between two hundred and three hundred cases of suicide detailed in English rolls, the Devil is explicitly blamed for the event in at least five cases (*per instigationem diaboli*), "at the instigation of the devil."[11] Tolkien subtly allows Sauron to play the same role in Denethor's fall. Step by inexorable step, Sauron twists the steward's perceptions and leads him to one mistaken conclusion after another, until at last he sees no way out. Instead of resisting the five temptations listed in the *ars moriendi*—failure of faith, despair, impatience, complacence, and avarice—Denethor yields to every one. The narrator in the appendix reveals how the ongoing contest of wills between the Lord of Minas Tirith and the Lord of Barad-dûr increases both pride and despair in Denethor: pride, because he is able to resist, and despair because he sees the armies of Sauron building (*LR,* 1031). Selfish as he is, the steward does not think to look beyond his own borders or ask for help; he sees the battle as a challenge to Gondor alone. He is unwilling to believe in the worthiness of anyone other than himself, or even that anyone else is capable of resisting the Enemy. Instead of waiting for death to come in its own time, he insists that it will come at a time of his choosing. He is willing to let others die and shirks his duties as leader, and above all, he will not let go of his last remaining tie to Middle-earth, his son Faramir. Any of these failures is lamentable, but taken all together, they equal a horrendous display of arrogance, betrayal, and destruction.

For this reason, pride and despair are necessarily linked. One inevitably

leads to the other. Denethor links the two: "Pride and despair!" he shouts
at Gandalf, defying both the messenger and the message that might otherwise save him (*RK,* V, vii, 835). Both are centered on the self; pride asserts,
"I can do all things," while despair laments, "I can do nothing." They mark
outermost ends of the spectrum of human potential. While most people
manage a respectable balance, Denethor has become unhinged enough that
he vacillates wildly; the center cannot hold. Only at the moment of his
death does he at last give voice to the twisted perceptions of reality and
the corrupting manipulations of the Enemy. In his last moment, he finally
rejects humility and service, and, above all, hope: hope that Sauron might
yet be defeated, hope that the King might return, hope that all this suffering might yet have meaning. For this reason, despair was considered a
terrible sin in the Middle Ages: it meant a lack "not just of Hope, but also
of Faith"—an implicit rejection of the idea that there might be anything
deeper or higher than human experience. Hence, despair could be used as
a synonym for suicide, one of the great moral stigmas of the middle ages:
people who elected to kill themselves were "guilty of a particular sin, an
especially deadly one, despair" to such an extent that "words like *dispera-*
zione and *despespoir* could often actually mean suicide, a usage that had the
double advantage of euphemism and of joining the unmentionable act with
a known—and unmentionable—sin."[12] It is the ultimate failure of faith.
Denethor has abandoned any hope for the future, and any faith that things
might turn out right after all. When Gandalf sacrificed himself for his
friends and died, it was with the hope that someone else could complete his
task; when Denethor prepares to die, it is with the belief that no one will.
He wants things to remain the same or, if that proves impossible, to have
nothing at all (*RK,* V, vii, 836). As Richard Purtill points out, "This is the
true voice of pride: either things as *I* want them or nothing. It is the voice
of the spoiled child, the adult egomaniac, the sinner who will not repent."[13]
Denethor has a choice, and he chooses despair. Despite Gandalf's plea to
leave the pyre and take part in the defense of the city, the steward refuses,
throws himself on a pyre, and immolates himself.

All deaths are painful, but Denethor's is particularly harsh. Instead of
the valor of Théoden or the penitence of Boromir, we are left only with
the bitter aftertaste of pride and needlessness. It is easy to see why medieval people regarded suicide with such horror. For in the end, Denethor's

grand gesture of defiance accomplishes nothing good. Théoden dies because Gandalf is distracted, murder is committed on sacred ground, and both Gondor and Rohan lose their rulers in a single day. But while Théoden's death elicits deep mourning on the part of his survivors, Denethor's passing evokes, so far as we are told, only a momentary grief.[14] Aragorn, Gandalf and the other princes immediately take up the governance of the city, and Faramir never mentions his father again. All Denethor's subtle counsels are simply set aside. Even the *palantír* is rendered useless. No one can look in it again, for unless they are very strong of will they see nothing but an old man's hands, withering in flame.

Flame of a far more dramatic fashion ends Gollum's life. But there is a certain balance in the way the two characters meet their ends. That which Denethor covets can be ended with ordinary fire, but the object of Gollum's desire can only be destroyed in the volcanic fires of Mt. Doom. If Denethor's death serves as a warning against the dangers of pride and despair, Gollum's likewise works as a caution against the dangers of covetousness. Throughout the course of *The Lord of the Rings,* "the driving force of his existence is his attempt to get the Ring back," and he has no purpose or direction without it.[15] Yet the Ring is also his prison; it is the encompassing, perpetual circle from which he cannot escape, an endlessly continuing zero. With it, he will not age and does not die, but neither can he grow: nothing much that's new happens to him. In fact, Gollum's prolonged existence beneath the Misty Mountains has given him many of the traits associated with the Old Norse "after-walkers" (*aptgangr*) or living dead—characteristics Tolkien certainly would have recognized even if he didn't deliberately set out to link them to Gollum.

As Nancy Caciola points out, belief in living corpses was widespread throughout Northern Europe, occurring in Brittany, France and Germany as well as England, Scotland, and Iceland.[16] The most famous examples, of course, derive from Norse *aptgangr* or "afterwalkers," more generally knows as the *haugbúi* (pl. *haugbúar*) and *draugr* (pl. *draugar*) who "lived" in their burial mounds. These are very physical creatures, able to walk, talk, and interact with the living in quite material ways. Such troublesome corpses appear in everything from quasi-historical texts like the *Laxdæla saga* to the rather more fanciful *Eyrbyggja saga.* As a general rule, those who were nastier individuals in life tend to become *aptgangr* in death; with a few exceptions, good people generally tend to stay dead. Those who do walk after death, however, make nuisances of themselves at best and become downright dangerous at worst: the *draugr* Thorolf kills several innocent people and, vampire-like, makes them *draugr* like himself until his son Arnkel puts a stop to it. When Arnkel dies, however, the haunting starts again.[17]

Gollum, of course, is very much alive, but like other creatures associated with the Ring, he has ended up in a sort of shadowy half-life, where a good deal of the person he once was, and almost all of the person he might have been, is lost. Even in *The Hobbit,* Gollum is described as "dark as darkness, except for two big round pale eyes in his thin face" (71). Tolkien later said that the darkness might have referred to Gollum's rags, not his skin, but in this instance the narrator really can have it both ways: the Old Norse *aptgangr* can be either *hel-blár,* "black as hell," or *ná-folr,* "corpse pale."[18] The shining eyes have their precedent one of the most famous of all the *aptrgangar,* the *draugr* Glamr of *Grettir's Saga:* the sight of Glamr's eyes shining in the moonlight terrifies Grettir more than anything else.[19] In *The Lord of the Rings,* Tolkien has made Gollum even more *draugr*-like: he is "a thieving, kin-murdering, treasure-hoarding, sun-hating, underground dweller who ought to be dead," but his continued presence among the living is both poignant and edifying.[20] The Ring may provide extended life, but it also makes Gollum one of the quasi-undead. Unless one happens to be an Elf, the experience of living necessarily pushes one closer to dying, and Tolkien makes it clear that that is how it should be.

To be fair, immortality was never Gollum's goal. As Gandalf tells it, in his youth the young proto-hobbit longed not for eternal life or great power or even treasures but for knowledge. No student, scholar, or scientist can fault him for that. He wanted to get at the roots of things, to understand how they worked (*FR,* I, ii, 51). Perhaps if he had begun his tenure with the Ring in a more auspicious way—with mercy or kindness, like Bilbo— things might have turned out differently. Probably not: even Bilbo, Gandalf suggests, would have fallen under the pull of the Ring eventually, and Gollum has held the Ring (or the Ring has held him) for five hundred years. But, in any case, Sméagol did not begin his ownership with mercy or kindness: his first act upon seeing the Ring was to murder his best friend. Throughout his long and unnatural life, Gollum is haunted by the knowledge that he gained the Ring only through Déagol's death. Over the years, he has made up a defense for his actions that, like the Ring itself, goes in endless circles without arriving anywhere. His attempts to justify his claim on the Ring are questionable at best and no more convincing to us than they are to him. At some level—the hobbit part, the part that has not quite surrendered to the Ring—Gollum has retained enough of his mortal morality to know that murdering Déagol was wrong. But, having begun, Sméagol cannot turn back, and his actions from that point forward become increasingly deceitful, petty, and malicious. As he slowly succumbs to the power of the Ring, "we witness a degeneration from curiosity," which is good, "to furtive, isolated seeking," which leads to nothing but trouble.[21]

As all readers know, Gollum eventually makes his way to the cave under the Misty Mountains, and there he remains until the day Bilbo Baggins finds the Ring. After that, Gollum has to leave; the need for the Ring compels him. Eventually, he makes his way to Mordor, where Sauron tortures him to reveal what he knows about the location of the One Ring. What happens afterward is not quite clear, though Frodo and Aragorn both suspect Gollum did not so much escape from Mordor as get released in order to accomplish further mischief on Sauron's behalf. But even under threat of further torture, and despite promises extracted and orders given, Gollum still plans to keep the Ring—and not out of any altruistic purpose, like Frodo, but simply because he wants the Ring for himself. In contrast to Gandalf's willingness to sacrifice even his own life to ensure the Ring is destroyed stands Gollum's determination to do all he can do preserve both the Ring and his own precious skin.

Still, even after five hundred years, Sméagol is not completely lost. Fragments of the proto-hobbit that he was break through, often at critical moments. He leads Frodo and Sam faithfully through the Dead Marshes, even rescuing Frodo (or, more cynically, the Ring) from the tainted water. He does not betray the hobbits to the forces of the Enemy, even given numerous opportunities. And, most powerfully of all, he almost repents on the stairs of Cirith Ungol:

> Gollum looked at them. A strange expression passed over his lean hungry face. The gleam faded from his eyes, and they went dim and grey, old and tired. . . . Then he came back, and slowly putting out a trembling hand,

very cautiously he touched Frodo's knee—but almost the touch was a caress. For a fleeting moment, could one of the sleepers have seen him, they would have thought that they beheld an old weary hobbit, shrunken by the years that had carried him far beyond his time, beyond friends and kin, and the fields and streams of youth, an old starved pitiable thing. (*TT,* IV, viii, 699)

It is a poignant moment, rich with possibility and pathos—until Sam wakes up. With Sam's accusations, whatever was left of Sméagol crumbles away. He can still call himself by that name, but it no longer fits. He starts referring to himself exclusively in the third person again. Gollum shows no more remorse, no more hesitation, no more pity—and it will lead him to his doom.

Though his inevitable end has been forecast throughout the story, the actual moment still comes as something of a shock. Whatever else the reader might have imagined Gollum's fate would be, falling to a fiery death in an active volcano still surprises first-time readers. But, as Gandalf says, "a traitor may betray himself and do good that he does not intend" (*RK,* V, iv, 797). For, in the ultimate twist of fate, it is Gollum, not Frodo, who finally destroys the Ring. In the pivotal moment, just before he ought to throw the Ring into the fires of Orodruin, Frodo at last succumbs to the pull of the Ring. Only two people are available to act at that point: Sam, too dazed to intervene, and Gollum, driven mad by his lust for the Ring. By some strange instinct, Gollum knows precisely where the Ring is, despite Frodo's invisibility; he rushes forward, attacks Frodo, and bites off the Ring with Frodo's finger still in it. But the Ring is the inevitable catalyst of Gollum's own destruction. Even as he falls into the fiery depths of Mount Doom, his thoughts are filled with the Ring: he cries out for it, and then he and the symbolic zero melt into nothing.

There is a fearful symmetry about Gollum's end, as if his fate and the Ring's were so intertwined that even their destruction could not be individual. By the time Frodo reaches Mount Doom, Gollum is entirely the Ring's creature; he has sacrificed the whole of himself to it, and nothing of the pitiable old hobbit remains. Thus, it is both just and fitting that "Gollum's desire for the ring leads to its destruction and his own"; he is in that moment utterly devoured by the Ring, and with the

Ring he is consumed.[22] Perhaps it could have happened no other way. Indeed, Frodo's failure and Gollum's role in the destruction of the Ring have been adumbrated from the very beginning of the story; Gandalf tells Frodo quite plainly that Gollum's fate is inevitably bound up with that of the Ring (*FR*, I, ii, 58). And part of that justice is that Gollum deserves his fiery end. He does not merit a heroic death; not repenting, he cannot die a penitent. His last act is one not of repentance or altruism but of injury and theft: he robs Frodo and permanently maims him. His last thoughts are not of atonement, nor even of the people or the world he leaves behind: he dies beseeching the One Ring to save him.

But in so doing, he saves Middle-earth. And so, beyond the sense that Gollum merits his fate is another kind of justice altogether: the painful recognition that death may be the kindest fate for Gollum. There is therefore in Gollum's moment of death a glimmer of hope: perhaps even he may be saved. But that lies beyond the scope of the book or even of Tolkien's own conception: "Into the ultimate judgement upon Gollum I would not care to enquire," he wrote. "This would be to investigate 'Goddes privitee,' as the Medievals said."[23] It may be that Gollum's fall into the Crack of Doom marks the most straightforward fall into Hell in the history of literature. However, since Tolkien was Catholic, a more optimistic interpretation allows the possibility that perhaps the fires of Orodruin mark Gollum's entrance into a kind of purgatory, in which even he may eventually be healed.

Gollum's death thus has about it the ineffable air of both justice and mercy. Justice, because he is a traitor several times over, a murderer and a thief; both Frodo and Gandalf agree that he deserves death. Usually, that statement is read as a condemnation, and when Frodo first utters it, he means it as such. But Gandalf, with the subtlety of a wizard, at once affirms Frodo's definition and simultaneously offers another. They both know, and so does that reader, that Gollum *should* have died hundreds of years ago; he *would* have died if the Ring had not crossed his path. No one considers falling into a volcano a good or noble end, and yet there is a sense in which Gollum's death is merciful: it ends a life that has gone on too long, that has lost all its meaning and purpose, and breaks the circle of enslavement and betrayal which has held Gollum for so long. "Deserves death" is not always an indictment.

Yet if death can be an instrument of mercy in some cases, it can be an instrument of justice in others. If, as Tolkien implies, Providence had a hand in Gollum's death, Saruman and Gríma die by direct human intervention.[24] The events that precede the deaths of Saruman and Gríma Wormtongue have been a long time coming, but they do not occur until the penultimate chapter of the book. When Frodo, Sam, Merry, and Pippin return home, they find that the Shire has been pillaged, polluted, and occupied by thugs. At first, they believe Frodo's cousin Lotho Sackville-Baggins is responsible, but it turns out that the mastermind behind the desecration of the Shire is none other than Saruman himself. Understandably, many of the hobbits wish to kill him, but Frodo stops them. He has endured much on his journey and has felt the terrible lure of evil. He knows the temptation to power.

For that is the sin to which Saruman and Gríma succumb, if sin it be. As Tom Shippey points out, there is nothing inherently wrong with the wish for power, although Carol Fry recently stated that the "desire for power is the core element of evil in Arda."[25] Perhaps it would be more accurate to say that the real danger lies in "getting above oneself"—not in the sense of social or political advancement, or Sam the Gardener would never have become Sam the Mayor or the "true hero" of *The Lord of the Rings*. Instead, it means avoiding self-centeredness or self-interestedness. There is nothing wrong with seeking power to correct the wrongs of the world or intending to use one's power to help others, but there is everything wrong with using one's power to shape the world according to one's own vision of how things ought to be. In the ordered world in which *The Lord of the Rings* takes place, all creatures have their place. This is not predestination, which allows no possibility for change or growth. It is instead what Paul Kocher called "Cosmic Order," which he defines as a "moral dynamism in the universe to which each of [the characters] freely contributes, without exactly knowing how, and without being at all sure how it will eventually work out."[26] To extend Tolkien's own metaphor, the world functions more like a musical composition. While some notes may be augmented or diminished, no one note is more important than any other, and even the discordant elements necessarily lend themselves to the final harmonies. Further, each note is unique even as it is part of the whole: middle C will always be middle C, but it will resonate and resound differently with different players, instruments, chords, silences. To work, though, it must remain itself.

The danger comes when somebody decides his or her part of the composition isn't big or grand or glorious enough. The dissonance begins with Melkor but then continues on throughout the history of Middle-earth. The *Ainulindalë* tells how the original music with which the fictive godhead Eru designed the universe was marred, and the echoes of that discord rumble throughout the rest of history. Melkor corrupts Sauron; Sauron corrupts Saruman; Saruman corrupts Gríma Wormtongue.

How exactly he accomplishes such a thing we will never fully know, but Gandalf makes it clear that Saruman promised Gríma two things: treasure and Éowyn. Neither was the former's to give or the latter's to take. Treasure belongs rightfully to the King, and while it is true that Éowyn might fulfill the *freoðuwebbe* (peaceweaver) role sometimes expected of Anglo-Saxon princesses, she does so entirely of her own free will, and there is no indication anywhere that Théoden or anyone else thinks of her as a commodity. She is entirely her own. But Gríma seeks to possess her, and somewhere therein lies his downfall. For whatever reason, he is someone she would not and did not consider. Perhaps he was not wellborn enough; perhaps he was not handsome enough. He was certainly not courageous enough. In a warrior culture like that of the Rohirrim, cowardice would be a great failing indeed. He may once have been a good man, but he clearly fears going to war: two times in the space of three paragraphs he pleads with Théoden not to send him to battle, and he cannot work up the courage to leave Saruman despite the abuse the wizard heaps upon him, even when others offer him shelter (*TT*, III, vi, 509, 510, 508). Only at the very last can he take action, but by then, it is fatal.

The exact nature of Saruman's fall, too, remains largely a matter of speculation. Clarifying the situation in a letter, Tolkien explains that part of the problem arises from simple impatience. Instead of waiting patiently for the designs of the Valar or Eru to come to pass, Saruman wanted to make things happen according to his agenda, which lead "to the desire to force others to [his] own good ends, and so inevitably at last to mere desire to make [his] own [will] effective by any means."[27] That is what makes the Ring so tempting: it offers, or seems to offer, a "quick fix" for the problem of evil. But forcing one's will on another is not good at all: it is slavery and rape. Gandalf and Galadriel both recognize the trap and turn away. Saruman does not and succumbs. He pretends to take the long view, claiming that he will bide his time until the day he can take the Ring from Sauron, but in reality he means to take the Ring for himself as soon as possible. The consequence, of course, is that he ends up serving Sauron in fact as well as in appearance. The Istari whom Gandalf once calls the greatest of his order becomes nothing more than a servant of a servant.

So matters stand when we first meet these characters, and their situation does not improve any as the story progresses. In fact, things rapidly begin to decline for them. Gríma loses his position at Théoden's court and becomes Saruman's lackey; Saruman becomes first a prisoner in his own home and then an exile from it, finally becoming a beggar on the road. All the vast power he once wielded as a Maia or a wizard seems to have left him completely: when he reaches the Shire, there is evidence of plenty of malice but little magic. He has sunk so low that the hobbits he once despised, literally the smallest people in Middle-earth, possess more than he. Even the power of his voice has dwindled: earlier, even the Riders who accompanied Théoden and Gandalf to confront Saruman were in danger from the mere sound of his voice. Now, eight months later, when Saruman tries to intimidate the hobbits with a curse on whoever spills his blood, Frodo is easily able to dispel the "spell." "He has lost all power," Frodo tells his fellows, "save his voice that can still daunt and deceive you, *if you let it*" (RK, VI, viii, 995; emphasis mine). This is a far cry from the voice that once had the power to enchant even those who stood on the edges of the spell. The terrible curse he utters—"if my blood stains the Shire, it shall wither and never again be healed"—proves completely ineffective (995). Saruman's blood does, in fact, stain the Shire, but the year that follows proves bountiful beyond all measure.

Saruman and Gríma both derive a large part of their power from speech, and as their power diminishes, so does their language. In fact, Gríma's nickname represents just the kind of philological game Tolkien loved to play; the connotations of the *wyrm* are, like Gríma himself, both subtle and threatening. In Old English, *wyrm* [Old Norse *orm*] means "worm," "serpent," or "dragon," and dragons, as the narrator of *The Hobbit* says, are known for their love of "riddling talk," and while Gríma did not precisely speak in riddles, he did use language to deceive his lord (221). For years, he has used his language—his tongue, meaning both his speech and the physical appendage used to express it—to deceive and control Théoden, until the old king is completely enthralled. Even against an adversary as formidable as Gandalf, Wormtongue's rhetorical skills are remarkable, and his spells so subtle, so gradual, that even members of Théoden's own household do not recognize them as *spells*. They seem to think his advice is only that: advice, albeit particularly bad and dangerous advice. But no one who speaks against him is successful until Gandalf breaks the spell.

Saruman's voice is even more deadly. It is a beautiful voice, "low and melodious, its very sound an enchantment" (*TT,* III, x, 564). Even to hear it can be dangerous: the narrator tells us that for some people, "the voice alone was enough to hold them enthralled," but "none were unmoved, none rejected its pleas and commands without an effort of mind and will" once they heard it (564). On the steps of Orthanc, the Riders hearing the voice suddenly believe Gandalf has been less than gracious to their King—and they are not even the ones to whom Saruman is speaking (565). Shortly later, even Théoden fears that Gandalf will betray them and go to consult with Saruman about "deep things beyond their comprehension" (567). Yet in the Shire, Frodo quickly renders Saruman's curse harmless. By then, Saruman's words have been reduced to the language of the churl; there is no poetry in it. His speech has gone from "Valour in arms is yours, and you win high honour thereby" to "Worm killed your Chief, poor little fellow, your nice little Boss" (*TT,* III, x, 566; *RK,* VI, viii, 996). Gone is the beautiful speech that tempted the wisest of souls; now there is only the coarse language of the thief. He can briefly mimic the high language he once spoke instinctively, but it no longer comes naturally.

Gríma, for his part, has been reduced from the counselor of a king to the bootlicker of a beggar. He says only eleven words during the entire conversation, and those he delivers in cringing monosyllables. Saruman has not been kind to him. Saruman is well-fed; Gríma is starving. Saruman lives in Bag-End; Gríma lives in a hut. Saruman walks; Gríma crawls. He is not even given the half-dignity of his full epithet: Saruman calls him "Worm" and orders him about "like a dog" (*RK,* VI, viii, 995, a comparison the narrator also uses). His very name emphasizes the change in status: he has gone from a man whose name suggested the insidious language of dragons to an animal that cannot speak or think at all. A worm can only act. And appropriately enough, what little exists of Gríma's speech suggests that even his actions are governed by Saruman's will: "You told me to; you made me do it" (996). Saruman does not deny it; he mocks Gríma yet again and kicks him in the face.

That is the critical moment that brings about Saruman's death. Gandalf spares Saruman twice, once at Orthanc and once on the Road back across the Mountains. Treebeard, who perhaps has better cause than any to wish the wizard dead, spares him too. Frodo spares him, even when Saruman tries to stab him with a hidden knife. But that last act of petty cruelty is too much for Gríma. Something in him finally snaps. He pulls out a knife, leaps unto Saruman's back, and cuts his master's throat. Moments later, as Wormtongue runs down the lane, he is shot by a number of hobbits and falls dead. So the lesser traitor brings down the greater, to the mutual destruction of both. Still, it's hard to blame Wormtongue for acting and easy to see his last act as the only heroic thing he ever accomplishes. For Gollum, the phrase "deserves death" indicates a release from a world in which he had lived far too long. For Saruman, the same phrase conveys justice, an appropriate response for a cruel individual who had done all he could to destroy others for his own ends. That it is Gríma Wormtongue who finally delivers the blow only strengthens the sense of justice. Their lives have been entwined from the moment Wormtongue gave his allegiance to Saruman; it is fitting that their deaths should be interwoven as well. As for Gríma's own passing, well, given that everything he had ever desired—the treasure of Rohan, the love of Éowyn, perhaps even the honor and respect of the Rohirrim—is now forever out of reach, death may have been the best option he could hope for. The justice of his death is beyond question. The suggestion of mercy, however, remains.

Still, it is worth noting that most of the wisest characters in *The Lord of the Rings* prefer mercy to justice. Hate engenders hate. Evil begets evil. Tolkien was not naive enough to believe that such method would always be effective, or Saruman would likely have gone on living. But he did allow that Frodo, at least, had "reached the conclusion that physical fighting is actually less ultimately effective than most (good) men think it!" as a solution to difficult problems.[28] In this situation, Frodo sought to find a workable balance between mercy and justice: letting Saruman live but sending him into exile in the hope that the wizard would grow great again. Exile may not be an easy punishment, but it does allow for the possibility of redemption.

Critics often remark on the inverse relationship between Théoden and Denethor, in which Théoden rises to greatness while Denethor descends to madness. But there is another, even more striking inverse relationship between Saruman and Frodo. The little hobbit has grown greater than the mightiest of the Istari, and Saruman knows it. It makes him hate Frodo all the more, and makes the gift of Frodo's mercy that much harder to bear. By all rights, Frodo ought to return to the Shire, be a hero for a little while, and then die, a mortal trapped in mortal lands. *Lif is læne,* after all, and all things under the sun must pass away. Saruman, by contrast, should have finished his task with honor and returned over the sea to Valinor. Instead, Saruman dies in the Shire, his body withers away, and Frodo makes the journey to Elvenhome. In his way, the little hobbit surpasses the greatest of the Istari. Frodo tries to show Saruman mercy, and in return, Saruman tries to kill him. He tries to show Wormtongue mercy, and Saruman's mockery of that mercy results in his own death.

But that is not the final word on Saruman's fate. Instead of lying perfectly still, as a well-mannered corpse ought to do, Saruman's death triggers another reaction: a grey mist gathers around the body, but a gust of wind comes out of the West and dissolves the mist into nothing (*RK,* VI, x, 997). His spirit may long to return to the light of Valinor and the lands beyond the Sea, but he cannot. Where he does go, we cannot say. However, it may be worth remembering that although Tolkien is accused of prejudice against the East, that is also the direction of awakenings and beginnings: Cuiviénen, the land where the Elves first awakened and began to speak, lies somewhere in the distant East. Maybe even the essence of Saruman will be given the chance to start anew. His body, however, is destroyed. The last image we have of it is not the peaceful sleep of death or even the ordinary unease caused by viewing a corpse, but a sort of quick-time movie where decomposition sets in at once, bringing the state of the body into alignment with the fate of the spirit. In the space of minutes or possibly even seconds, Saruman's face crumbles into nothing more than "rags of skin upon a hideous skull" (viii, 996–67). Justice has been done, and there is nothing more to do but bury the dead, and, as Sam points out, clean up the mess.

Those who meet bad deaths in *The Lord of the Rings* almost inevitably bring it upon themselves. Just like the heroes Sam speaks of, they had opportunities to turn back, to mend their ways, but they didn't. Gandalf reminds Denethor that there is still hope, that the King will come again; Denethor chooses stagnation. Gollum cannot let go of the lure of the Ring. Saruman and Gríma Wormtongue are given multiple chances to turn back; neither will. All any of them had to do to be saved was to let go, to stop clinging to pride or to envy or selfishness. The tympana over a number of medieval churches feature the condemned being lead off to Hell by means of a rope, but the rope does not bind them—even a cursory inspection of the images shows that the figures hold the rope tightly in their own hands. All any of the doomed need to do to escape their fate is *let go*. The message of the "bad" deaths in *The Lord of the Rings* is "not to keep hold but to let go, since there is no surety in clinging to any thing too long or too hard" in the mortal world.[29] The key word is "thing": tangible things will inevitably pass away. Ideals like love and friendship and freedom might lead to death, but a "good" death: these are the stars by which to light our way.

CHAPTER 3

Songs and Stones

The sheer number of deaths in *The Lord of the Rings* naturally inevitably leaves its mark on the landscape, forming part of the material evidence of the long history of Middle-earth. As the narrative progresses, the reader encounters the ruins of extinct empires, stands beside the memorials of long-dead warriors, and hears the tales of ancient heroes. In each case, someone speaks for the dead, telling their tales and remembering their deeds anew, so that their stories become part of the cultural identity of the peoples of Middle-earth, defining both individual cultures and the collective heritage of the free peoples. Seldom is any historical feature in Middle-earth found without an attendant song or story to explain its significance. The same process is even more pronounced when it comes to gravesites or memorials and the songs that accompany them. And so it is that "death is engraved on the landscape," marking the places, peoples, and cultures that once lived there and in some cases live there still.[1] Graves and memorials communicate history, heritage, and homeland; they assert that the past has happened and that it continues to exert its influence on the present. By their very nature, graves and monuments are deliberate interruptions of the landscape, one person's attempt to call attention to the former existence of another. They insist on explanation, and that requires that someone must know the stories that explain their presence. The stories, in turn, make the past "live again," giving it agency in the present and therefore the potential to be passed down into the future. The songs, in short, explain what the monuments mean.

The importance of the gravesite tends to be downplayed in contemporary societies; some movements advocate abandoning individually marked graves altogether or using a tree as a kind of surrogate headstone. But the placement of graves is rarely if ever random; instead, it results from "a conscious and carefully thought-out activity by which the dead are both remembered and forgotten, and through which we reaffirm and construct our attitudes to death and the dead and, through these, to place and identity."[2] For most of human history, graves were important not only as individual resting places but as boundary-markers, gathering-places, execution sites and legislative centers. Sometimes gravesites are feared, and sometimes they are hallowed, but in all cases they are "visible, visitable and verdant, a major proclamation of our ancestors."[3] Graves link past, place, and present; they are the material manifestation of memory and the physical assertion of existence.

Moreover, graves are deeply indebted to the cultures they commemorate. As Eva Reimers notes, "graveyards function as communicative symbolic practices that construct and express individual and collective ethnic and cultural identity."[4] Tombs raised to ancestors in Japan are distinctly different from those found in Europe; even within individual communities, burial preferences fluctuate over time. Styles change; materials become available or fade from popularity; elaborate carvings give way to simpler monuments and flow back again. In York, tombstones crafted in the tenth century blended both secular (folkloric) and spiritual (Christian) imagery, including dragons and other animals, while in Puritan America the winged death's-head gradually gave way to winged cherubs in a process almost cinematic in its progression.[5] Today, the flat headstones proliferating in lawn cemeteries everywhere suggest the desire to overlook death itself—although that belief, as we shall see in chapter 5, is oversimplified.

As it is in human societies, so it is in the imaginary places they create, and Middle-earth is no exception. Although each type of tomb has a parallel in the real world, each culture's monuments are subtly adapted to reflect the beliefs and customs of the people who made them. While "all the inhabitants of Middle Earth [sic], with the possible exception of the orcs, provide for the disposal of the dead by one means or another," each of the Three Kindreds shares the impulse to *bury* its dead.[6] While each of these practices is largely and naturally drawn from Tolkien's long

familiarity with the cultures of the Middle Ages, none are considered bar-
baric—perhaps because any practices he found distasteful were simply not
allotted to the peoples he created. Other forms of disposal, even those
described in Old Norse and Anglo-Saxon texts, are not found in Tolkien's legendarium—though they are occasionally mentioned. Cremations
are acceptable, if not desirable, especially in instances of dire need.[7] But
leaving the dead exposed to be eaten is seen as troublesome—even if the
dead are orcs—and no corpse is ever hung and left to rot in a tree. These,
too, were options available to Tolkien, even assuming he was deliberately
remaining within options available to him through the myths and legends
of Northern Europe. Yet he chose not to employ them. Instead, he gave
each of his cultures funereal traditions that are both distinct and common,
variations on a theme, allowing each one of his creations to claim its place
as the Children of Ilúvatar while maintaining a unique culture of its own.

The sole exception to the rule may be the Orcs, who may or may not
offer a darker alternative: cannibalism. "He might as well go in the pot,"
observes Gorbag, thinking the envenomed Frodo dead (*TT,* IV, x, 723).
Shagrat threatens to eat a rebel (*RK,* VI, i, 885). The Uruk-hai remain
loyal to Saruman in part because he gives them man's-flesh to eat (*TT,*
III, iii, 436). The association between Orcs and the dead makes a grim
kind of sense: their very name links Orcs to corpses, and Tolkien knew
it. The word *orcnéas* appears in *Beowulf* (1.112) and is generally translated
as something like "corpse from under the ground" or "evil spirits of the
dead." In his translation of *Beowulf,* Tolkien translates the word *orcnéas* as
"haunting shapes of hell" (l. 90–91 / 112) and provides a brief gloss in the
"Commentary" defining *Orcus* as "Hell, Death" (Orcus is actually a minor Latin deity of the underworld) and *né* as "dead body."[8] Many scholars
speculate that the word has roots in necromancy, whereby a malignant
individual would raise evil spirits by using corpses.[9] And, of course, in
The Hobbit Sauron is referred to as "the Necromancer," although the
goblins never threaten to eat Thorin and the Company (though that they
do eat ponies and other unspecified "dreadful things" is rather ominous).

For the most part, however, such a practice is so far removed from
the consciousness of the major characters that they hardly recognize it,
even when directly confronted with it; instead, it is just another aberra-
tion and corruption of the Orcs. All other peoples of Middle-earth bury

their dead in ways distinct to their specific cultures and that fulfill specific cultural demands. In this sense, gravestones constitute a kind of public performance; they are "public declarations of sorrow and respect" that "are meant as lasting elegiac 'performances,' acts to honor the dead."[10] All gravestones, by their very nature, invite the viewer to gaze upon them and interpret the deceased's life; even the most spare monuments usually include at least a name, birth and death dates, and sometimes a fairly innocuous phrase giving that person's relationship to another person or family. For someone with the right training or inclination, tombstones sometimes can be read symbolically: "Dead men may tell no tales," notes Douglas Keister, "but their tombstones do."[11] A skull, for instance, signals death clearly enough, just as a cross indicates Christianity or a Star of David Judaism. One need not even be a Christian or a Jew to intuitively grasp at least this much about the person interred beneath the stone.

In Middle-earth, where the entire world is communicated solely by symbols—it has no existence of its own beyond marks on the page—Tolkien streamlines this process even more. A great deal about each culture can be inferred through its burial practices. Elves make monuments of ethereal grace and beauty, frequently in forests, as befits a race concerned with beauty and a reverence for nature. Dwarves construct tombs of stone, practical and durable, appropriate for a practical and durable people who mine the earth and live in mountains. The graves of Men are as adaptable as the race itself, each reflecting the subtle nuances of thought about death and the afterlife appropriate to the originating culture. The way these people live with the dead, therefore, marks something significant about their individual cultures, memories, and identities as unique and vibrant beings. The places of the dead, and the stories their people tell about those places, keep the past alive, help the living remember the past.

For centuries, history was transmitted not through written records—though written records and oral histories often functioned in tandem—but through songs and stories, spread throughout Europe by scops and bards who kept the memories of the past alive. Thus, "literature is culture's memory, not as a simple recording device but as a body of commemorative actions."[12] Some scholars have even argued that *all* literature is commemorative, recording the memory of departed heroes, lost cultures, and eras of human history that might otherwise have faded into oblivion. Sadly, we know very little about how these songs and stories were actually passed down through the ages; the lines between storytelling and singing were once far less distinct than they are today. In the *Kalevala*, for instance, "'speak' and 'sing' are often paired in a virtually interchangeable fashion," while in Old English, *leoð* and *fit* can mean both "song" and "story."[13] We cannot know, now, exactly how the now-separate concepts were linked in medieval minds: Tolkien points out that we know almost nothing of the way the old stories were "sung," and because of the way Old English verse is structured, he doubted it was "sung" in the modern sense.[14] We only know that somehow, songs and stories worked together to record the past. The songs and stories our ancestors sang thus functioned as a sort of verbal cenotaph that marked the place of the dead not in the landscape but within culture itself.

Of course, not all the songs in *The Lord of the Rings* or in the wider legendarium are elegiac, and the story would be a good deal poorer if they were. Sam's song of the trolls might be called faintly elegiac, recalling as it does the loss of Tom's uncle's shinbone, but the overall tone is comic rather than funereal, even though it does involve a graveyard (*FR*, I, xiii, 201–3). And of course the extended fairy-tale rhyme of "The Man in the Moon" is delightfully whimsical.[15] But perhaps these are the kinds of songs that hobbits sing; Pippin later tells Denethor that hobbits seldom sing songs of anything more terrible than bad weather, which is, perhaps, telling enough about hobbit culture (*RK*, V, iv, 789). Hobbits clearly know the old legends and tales, but it is not at all clear precisely how they are passed down from generation to generation. Sam speaks of stories told by the fireside, so perhaps the best and most exciting stories are transmitted in that way, but it may also be that the duller or longer bits of history are recorded in books. The hobbits have a precise legal code in any case, and Bilbo, Sam, and Frodo carefully record their adventures in the Red Book (*FR*, I, i, 38).[16] But the Gaffer speaks suspiciously of literacy, and most hobbits seem content to pass along their traditions mostly by oral means. Memories of the heroic history of Middle-earth are not forgotten, but they are subsumed into more local, parochial concerns, like one's family genealogy or the history of Old Toby.

In fact, the only hobbit song that deals with death overtly is remarkable in that it looks *forward* in time, not backward. While sitting in Imladris waiting for the Company to begin their quest, Bilbo sings a quiet, retro-spective song, looking back over the ordinary experiences and everyday places the singer has known. These are not the heroic deeds that occupy the other songs of Men in Middle-earth; it is a quiet, simple reflection on a life—the narrator's life—thinking about the things he (or she) has seen and the things he will never have the opportunity to see. Although Tolkien never says so directly, the implication is clear: human beings do not live long enough to see and do all the things we would like to see and do, even if those things are as simple as seeing the woods turn green next spring. Because the song is sung in the Last Homely House, a place inhabited primarily by immortal Elves, the song's message is especially poignant. The speaker acknowledges that only in passing is he part of the long chain of humanity reaching down from the distant past and extend-ing on into the future. And then the song returns to the present, listening for the voices and footsteps that mark the sounds of everyday existence.

And for the most part, everyday life is precisely the kind of thing that hobbit-songs concern themselves with: walking and bathing and drinking and eating. But beyond the borders of the Shire, the hobbits encounter the deep history of Middle-earth, and much of that history is conveyed in song. In fact, the hobbits do not even need to leave the Shire to find it: their second night out from Bag-end, Frodo, Sam, and Pippin encounter Gildor and a band of wandering Elves, Exiles who still sing of Elvenhome and the wonders of the land they have lost. Already, the three hobbits hear echoes of a heroic age that has long gone by and can never be regained. The meaning of that song becomes clearer as the narrative progresses, until we at last reach Rivendell and hear the full story told by Elrond himself.

Small wonder, then, that Bilbo has begun to think about the world and his own small place within it. Because he is a hobbit, his song does not quite take on the epic scope or profound mourning of the Elvish elegies or the Mannish epics, but some awareness of the passing of time has begun to creep in. He has been surrounded by tales and songs of these ancient times and living among people like Elrond, something of a living relic in his own right. Elrond remembers the great army of Gil-galad and Elendil, who had previously been mentioned only in song. Rivendell seems to have at least one library, but it is also a place filled with songs, many of which are about the events from the distant past and the losses the Elves have suffered over the years (*FR*, II, iii, 270). In this way, the immortal Elves establish a link with the younger races: they know, just like Gimli does, that "memory is not what the heart desires" (viii, 369). They know what it is to die; they have felt the pain caused by death. From the tale of Beren and Lúthien on down to the song of Amroth and Nimrodel—even the snippet of *The Fall of Gil-galad*—the Elves share their culture and their loss through music. In their songs, they keep the memory of their past alive, transmit their own history to the younger races, and share in the pain of death and loss characteristic of all races of Middle-earth. And, like so many other songs in Tolkien's legendarium, they are commonly linked to the tangible markers of the past: ruins of buildings or graves and monuments for the dead.

The oldest graves in Middle-earth, appropriately enough, belong to the Firstborn Elves. Though they are intended to be immortal, they can die of grief or calamity, and while their spirits may go to dwell in the Halls of Waiting, their bodies clearly require different treatment. For the most part, the Elves seem to prefer mound burials, such as were raised over the Elvish heroes like Finduilas or Glorfindel (*Silm*, 216, 245). Finrod Felagund, too, is given a mound burial, although he seems to have been buried on a hilltop: a natural mound (175). But while such graves might presumably be found all over the map, only one Elvish monument is depicted in *The Lord of the Rings:* Cerin Amroth. Unlike the mounds of Glorfindel and Finrod, however, Cerin Amroth is a memorial and not yet a grave. Its eponymous builder, Amroth, made the mound and its crowning *flet* as a means of keeping watch over Dol Guldur, although a story in *Unfinished Tales* states that he may have adapted the idea from his beloved Nimrodel.[17] Neither of them is buried there, however. Before the Company comes to the foot of Cerin Amroth or even knows of its existence, Legolas sings "The Lay of Nimrodel," which tells the story of Amroth and Nimrodel. "It is long and sad," he tells his companions, because although the pair agreed to sail together to Valinor, both were lost in the attempt, and no one knows for certain what happened to either of them (*FR*, II, vi, 333). Nimrodel disappeared in the mountains somewhere between Lothlórien and the Bay of Belfalas, and

> Where she wanders none can tell
>> In sunlight or in shade;
> For lost of yore was Nimrodel. (331)

Her beloved Amroth is already waiting for her aboard a ship, but during the night a storm comes up and drives the ship far from shore. When he awakes and sees the shoreline fading behind him, he dives into the sea in a desperate attempt to return to his beloved. The lay thus ends with the hollow quatrain

> But from the West has come no word
>> And on the Hither Shore
> No tidings Elven-folk have heard
>> Of Amroth evermore. (332)

Part of the tragedy of the story is that the Elves do not *know* what happened to either Amroth or Nimrodel. Nimrodel was most likely killed in the mountains and Amroth drowned in the sea, but neither is certain. Because Elves are hardier than human beings and do not die unless slain or worn away by grief, it is possible—just—that Amroth and Nimrodel were reunited somewhere else on Middle-earth and have simply not made their way home again. For human beings, who know they will ultimately and finally be sundered from the people whom they love, this kind of ambiguity is almost impossible to bear. For Elves, who are intended by Eru to be immortal, and who know the fate of their dead when it does occur, this kind of unknowing must be almost unendurable. The only possible way to cope in the face of such a loss is to try to contain it, either in the material form of a memorial or in the metonymic form of a song. The peoples of Middle-earth quite frequently do both. "If made things reflect their makers, that reflection is memory"; and so the mound itself has become a monument to the past even as it continues to serve the purpose for which it was originally intended.[18] And indeed the "Lay of Nimrodel" is not mentioned again, but it does not need to be: the hobbits (and the reader) already know the story.

Like all things Elvish, Cerin Amroth is structurally simple, but elegant and filled with meaning. The memorial is closely allied with nature, a structure appropriate for a people so profoundly connected to the natural world. It is a great symmetrical grassy mound surmounted by a double crown of trees. The outer trees are of an unspecified species; their boles and limbs are white and leafless, but beautiful nonetheless. The inner trees are *mallorn,* the mystical trees unique to Lothlórien, with silver bark and golden leaves that do not fall until the new blooms of spring replace them.[19] At the top of a towering tree at the summit and center of the mound is a white *flet,* down below, flowers grow among the green grass at the roots of the trees: the golden, star-shaped *elanor* or the pale *niphredil* (*FR,* II, vi, 341).[20] Winter may reign elsewhere in Middle-earth, but Cerin Amroth echoes the springtime.

The memorial is dedicated more to memory than commemoration; it is a memorial, not a tomb, and the individual whose name it bears is not there. Indeed, the entire structure seems to be not so much a monument to Amroth as a visible mnemonic, meant not so much a means to honor a fallen king as a means of recalling the glories of the past to mind and so to keep them vibrant and alive. For the people of Lórien, who in their own tongue name themselves the Galadhrim, or "tree-people," the trees of Cerin Amroth are also an expression of cultural identity. Though the Elves of Middle-earth live in a variety of habitations, from palaces to houses to caves, the people of Lórien live among the trees; their lives and identities are bound to that of the forest they inhabit. Moreover, the *mallorn* are distinctly *Elvish* trees and flowers: they appear nowhere else on Middle-earth, and the perception is that they will fade when the Elves pass away. Galadriel's gift of a *mallorn* seed takes root in the Shire, where it too will become something of a monument, "the only *mallorn* west of the Mountains and east of the Sea" (*RK,* VI, ix, 1000). The implication is that it will stand long after Sam has crossed the Sea and the Elves have also passed away, a mute but beautiful testimony to days long past.

Even in the Primary World, trees are rich with symbolism; they have a long association with graves, monuments, and memorials. On the one hand, they are symbols of life and longevity; after all, some species live for thousands of years, and "there is that about trees which speaks of a powerful sense of life that endures."[21] Their longevity naturally suggests a sense of continuity; the tree planted by one's grandmother might well be the one under which one's grandchildren play. In England, yew trees in particular are commonly found around cemeteries; the yew's extreme longevity and ability of revive from the root makes it "one of the most powerful symbols of resurrection and eternal life."[22] In biblical imagery, too, trees were associated with immortality; the Tree of Life in particular was said to grant life eternal. On the other hand, eating from the Tree of the Knowledge of Good and Evil ultimately brought death into the world. Some traditions maintain that trees are planted in cemeteries because their complex root structure holds the dead down. In Old Norse mythology, the World Tree Yggdrasil raises its limbs in the realm of the gods, but spreads its roots in the land of the dead (*hel*); while *The Dream of the Rood* describes Christ's place of execution specifically as a tree (*trēow*, ll. 14, 25), a gallows (*gealgan*, l.40) and finally a gallows-tree (*gealgtrēow*, l. 145). As Andrew Reynolds points out, the Blickling Homilist of the later tenth century uses the same word; he applies the term *rode-galgan* for Christ's execution site, which William Morris translated for the Early English Texts Society as "rood-tree."[23] Eerily, British folklore sometimes regards trees as natural shelters for the souls of the departed.[24]

But the overall effect of Cerin Amroth is not frightening; it is "haunting, sad, and yet not unconsoling."[25] In fact, its connection to the past is its most striking attribute. Normal rules of time and space seem distorted: in the present, Frodo sees the past, the present, and the future, and not necessarily in that order. The site somehow seems to focus various perceptions of time itself, allowing "contrasting concepts of time: as both fluid and static, linear and circular, mortal and immortal."[26] It brings the past into the present: Frodo, stepping on the grass, seems to return to a time when the earth was new and all things were likewise new and wonderful. Colors appear fresh and vivid; he feels for the first time a delight in a tree as a tree, for its own sake; he hears the cry of birds that have long been extinct (*FR*, II, vi, 342). When he returns to the ground, he finds Aragorn standing at the base of the tree, lost in memory, looking as if the years had fallen away and he has grown young again. In a flash of insight, Frodo realizes that here, too, he sees things "as they once had been in this same place." As for Aragorn, his memory is so real, so powerful, that he speaks to someone who is not even there (341). But the last words of that chapter project the reader momentarily forward in time: recovering from his memory, Aragorn speaks words that may be prophetic: he tells Frodo that his heart will dwell there forever. Perhaps he speaks only of the compelling beauty of the place; Tolkien conceded that even in the Primary World "the heart remains in the description of Cerin Amroth," and so Aragorn might only mean that he will cherish the memory of meeting Arwen there forever.[27] But it could be prophetic in another way: in the "Tale of Aragorn and Arwen," we learn that long after the events in *The Lord of the Ring* become history, and King Elessar has passed away, Arwen makes her way back to Cerin Amroth—and there she dies (*LR,* 1038). In this reading, Aragorn's words become prophetic: the woman he loves, the lady to whom he has given his heart, will die there, and thus Cerin Amroth will eventually become a grave (1038). But that is in the distant future, and beyond the bounds of the story itself. Yet even the final words of the chapter move forward in time: they tell the reader that Aragorn will never return to Cerin Amroth as a living man (*FR,* II, vi, 343).

Like the Elves, Cerin Amroth is both outside of time and within it, magical yet natural, filled with a sense of longing and waiting, yet not without hope. What is traditionally a place of fear or sorrow for humanity is a place of remembrance and renewal for the Elves. Nevertheless, its role is important for the Company, and especially Frodo. The events on the mound are of singular consequence: it is there, for the first time, that Frodo realizes the full significance of his quest, not just for himself but for all the Free Peoples. As memorials are intended to, Cerin Amroth represents something larger than itself, a reminder of the transience of life, maybe, but also a permanent attestation to the power of memory.

In Moria, too, we are permitted to see only a single grave, and like Cerin Amroth it speaks to the nature of the people who created it. Though Tolkien acknowledged that the Dwarves of Middle-earth "are not quite the dwarfs of better known lore," he knew that they were more deeply indebted to tradition than the Eldar.[28] In the Germanic stories, dwarfs are consistently portrayed as highly skilled craftsmen—there are no female dwarfs—associated from the beginning with mines, mountains, metalwork, and stone. In the *Younger* or *Prose Edda,* Snorri Sturluson records how the dwarfs "had taken shape first and acquired life in the flesh of Ymir and were then maggots, but by decision of the gods they became conscious with intelligence and had the shape of men though they live in the earth and in rock."[29] He then cites several passages from the *Voluspá* illustrating their origins, including the oft-cited list of names from which Tolkien drew so many of the names of his characters, including Durin, the father of Dwarves, Ori (who recorded the last desperate entry in the Book of Records in Moria), and Glóin, Gimli's father and Bilbo's companion in *The Hobbit*. The dwarfs are not necessarily evil, but they are frequently treacherous and untrustworthy in their almost relentless pursuit of material gain. In Tolkien's mythology, too, the dwarves were originally almost always evil, as Christopher Tolkien notes in *The Book of Lost Tales*.[30]

But as Tolkien's mythology evolved, the Dwarves gradually became less repugnant, and in his two finished stories of Middle-earth almost nothing of their original, active malice is left. In *The Hobbit,* the narrator concedes that "dwarves are not heroes, but calculating folk with a great idea of the value of money; some are tricky and treacherous and pretty bad lots; some are not, but are decent enough people like Thorin and Company, if you don't expect too much," but they make the right decision in the end; in other words, they are a lot like people (211). By the time *The Lord of the Rings* came out twenty years later, their gold-lust has almost slipped into the background: it exists only in association with Moria, a place beset with dangers and missteps for anyone who enters. Their reasons for wishing to retake Moria are complex: at the Council of Elrond, Glóin speaks of a "shadow of disquiet" the fell on the Dwarves of the Lonely Mountain, a feeling that "greater wealth and splendour" could be had by returning (*FR,* II, ii, 234). Later in the Council, he even admits that Balin hoped to recover one of the Seven Rings of the Dwarves (261).

These are traditional motivations for Dwarves, and no one gives them a second thought. Gimli, however, provides a clue for a deeper meaning about the significance of Moria for the Dwarves. As is the case with Cerin Amroth, the full significance of Khazad-dûm is revealed only in a song. Just before the tomb of Balin is discovered, Gimli sings the "Song of Durin," in its own way a lament of the downfall of the dwarves from their high halls of Moria. The song begins with the commemoration of an individual:

> When Durin woke and walked alone.
> He named the nameless hills and dells;
> He drank from yet untasted wells;

. . . .
A king he was on carven throne
In many-pillared halls of stone
With golden roof and silver floor,
And runes of power upon the door. (*FR,* II, iv, 308)

The song depicts Moria as it once was, filled with images of material wealth
and power. As the song continues, though, it depicts Dwarves doing what
Dwarves do best: hammering, chiseling, forging, delving. It moves from
the commemoration of an individual to a lament for a way of life that can
never be again. The "Song of Durin" underscores what Michael D. C.
Drout calls "the lost-ness, the permanent separation from all that has come
before."[31] How appropriate, then, that the song ends with silence and the
image of a tomb:

No harp is wrung, no hammer falls:
The darkness dwells in Durin's halls;
The shadow lies upon his tomb
In Moria, in Khazad-dûm. (*FR,* II, iv, 308–9)

Small wonder that Balin and his folk wish to retake Moria. The al-
ways-powerful allure of glory and material gain are overlain with powerful cultural and historical motivation. It is the ancestral home of the
Longbeards and the resting place of their most important forefather. It
is the source of their greatest wealth, but beyond that it is starting point
for their culture in Middle-earth, the site of their greatest achievement,
and the location of their ancestral tombs. It would be something like
knowing where Adam and Eve first woke up *and* where their bones are
buried. Like Adam, Durin is even credited with naming things, much as
the Elves did when they first woke up. Furthermore, the Dwarves believe
Durin will be reincarnated seven times; between each incarnation, he
"sleeps" (*LR,* 1045–46). In fact, Tolkien eventually decided Durin VI was
the last king in Moria; he was slain by the Balrog and his people driven
away. The Dwarves had tried to retake Moria once before, when Thráin
son of Thrór led a host against the Orcs of Khazad-dûm in vengeance

for the slaying and desecration of his father. The War culminated in the
Battle of Azanulbizar, wherein so many Dwarves were slaughtered that
"their dead were beyond the count of grief," and though the Dwarves
won they were too few to keep and hold Moria again (1049). Still, the
Dwarves held that Durin VII would come from the line of Dain II, and
he would ultimately lead the Dwarves back to Moria.[32]

The sheer number of dead at the Battle of Azanulbizar interfered with
normal Dwarvish burial practices: there were simply too many to bury
properly. The stone tombs required by tradition would have taken too long
to build. Therefore, they turned to fire; they built pyres and burned all
the bodies of their kindred rather than leave the corpses to lie as carrion.
Perhaps in an attempt to reconcile what was considered a disgraceful end,
the Dwarves honored those who fell in Azanulbizar in memory, and "a
Dwarf will say proudly of one of his sires: 'he was a burned Dwarf,' and that
is enough" (LR, 1050). Traditionally, though, Dwarves bury their dead in
stone tombs, not in the earth, a practice distinct from both Elves and Men.
The emphasis on the materiality of the Dwarves, then, extends from their
cultural habits and mores in life straight into their physical and spiritual
beliefs at death. Christopher Tolkien even adds that "the flesh of Dwarves
is reported to have been far slower to decay or become corrupted than that
of Men."[33] Little is known of the tomb structure, however. A footnote in
appendix A notes that their location is secret and that Dwarves "lay their
dead only in stone not in earth," believing that they were made from stone
and will return to stone (LR, 1050n). This idea seems a clear allusion to
the Old Norse Alvíssimál, in which the dwarf Alvis is turned to stone in the
end.[34] Early drafts seem to suggest that the Dwarves had no souls at all;
but Thorin Oakenshield's dying proclamation that he goes to wait beside
his fathers—a statement not dissimilar to the dying words of Théoden
King—flatly contradicts that belief (Hobbit, 288).[35] The Silmarillion states
the Dwarves' belief that their souls would return to Aulë, who would give
them their own place in the halls of Mandos to await the end of time (44).
Later writings further complicate the picture: in "On Dwarves and Men,"
Tolkien played with the idea that a dead dwarf would "lie in a tomb of his
own body." The text seems to suggest death was a deeply meditative state
where the hurts of the flesh could be healed, after which the spirit could

return.[36] The need to recapture Moria thus takes on an urgency that would not be clear or obvious to outsiders: if the spirit of one's ancestor was going to return to or remain in that ancestor's physical remains, one would *not* want those remains to be in the keeping of Orcs and Balrogs.

All of this is highly speculative, building on ideas Tolkien only introduced in 1969 or later, and in any case, the option of reincarnation was available only to the forefathers. Beyond that, Tolkien did not say much about the actual burial practices of the Dwarves, which is perhaps fitting of a race that is secretive by nature. Only three Dwarven tombs are mentioned throughout the Legendarium: Durin's (though it must be accompanied by those of the other Durins, not to mention other inhabitants of Moria), Thorin Oakenshield's, and Balin's. Of them all, only Balin's is described in any detail.[37] As is the case with Cerin Amroth, it is rich with elements of the fictional culture that gave it birth. But in contrast to the "secret tombs of kings" otherwise located somewhere in Moria, the tomb of Balin is easy to find, in the Chamber of Mazarbul: "The chamber was lit by a wide shaft high in the further eastern wall; it slanted upwards and, far above, a small square patch of blue sky could be seen. The light of the shaft fell directly on a table in the middle of the room: a single oblong block, about two feet high, upon which was laid a great slab of white stone" (*FR*, II, iv, 311). Technically, Balin's is a chest tomb, so named because it looks like a rectangular chest with an epitaph carved onto its flat top. In the Primary World, these tombs began appearing roughly in the second quarter of the thirteenth century, although Balin's apparently lacks the arcading and other elaborate carving commonly seen on its medieval equivalents.[38] Although chest tombs look like they might contain bodies, they are usually empty; the body is actually buried beneath the tomb and not in it. And in fact, Gandalf later states that "Balin is buried deep" (v, 319). Thus, like other chest tombs, Balin's serves as a kind of elaborate marker of the burial space rather than as a coffin. But it is a distinctly Dwarvish chest tomb; although the Dwarves are master stonemasons, the monument is hard and bare, appropriate to a people who live and work among unyielding stone. Its lines are plain and angular; no elaborate carving decorates the sides of the tomb; no sculptural elements set it apart. The runes on the white stone mark the name and rank of the fallen, and that is all.

ᚱᚾᚻᛁᚢ

ᚴᛂᚲᛁᚢᛂᚠ

ᛂᛡᚱᚾᚠᚻᚾᛡᚾᚠᚠᚷᛒᛂ

ᚱᚾᚻᛁᚢᚲᛁᚢᛡᛋᛂᚲᛁᚢᚠᛡᛏᛂᛡᛒᛡᛏᚾ

The runes say only "Balin son of Fundin, Lord of Moria." The grave is not anonymous, but it is unremarkable, set off as belonging to somebody special only by its location. Like other Dwarvish burials depicted in Tolkien's published works—the burial of Thorin Oakenshield in *The Hobbit* being the other obvious example—Balin lies deep within the heart of the mountain. But while the precise location of Thorin's burial chamber remains unspecified, Balin is given a place within the Chamber of Records, the room that houses the written memory of his people. And memory is precisely what his tomb evokes: Gimli, in his grief, casts his hood over his face, and Frodo, who never knew Balin, finds himself nevertheless thinking of Bilbo and his adventures with the Dwarf (313).

Like other burials, Balin's tomb is intended to evoke emotion and remembrance, to recall the deeds of the dead and give the living a focus for their grief. But it also prompts the Company to begin searching "for anything that would give them tidings of Balin's fate, or show what had become of his folk" (*FR*, II, v, 313). The discovery of the tomb leads to the discovery of the Book of Records and thereby to the discovery of the ultimate fate of the Dwarves of Moria. Perhaps its placement in the midst of the Chamber of Mazarbul signals the Dwarves' awareness that their time in Moria was limited, and the stark monument bearing Balin's name nonetheless stands as a memorial for them all.

The monuments of the Elves and Dwarves, then, each reflect the cultures Tolkien imagined for them. The human societies depicted in *The*

Lord of the Rings, however, are much more heterogeneous, and this diversity is portrayed in their burial practices as well as in their mores and customs. In this carefully crafted world, built entirely from one man's imagination, the various means of disposal result from deliberate choices, dominated by distinctly medieval modes of burial that nevertheless seem familiar to modern audiences. In Gondor, for instance, people construct elaborate tombs reminiscent of late medieval effigies, while the mounds of Rohan echo those of people living in the early Middle Ages. Deliberately or not, then, Tolkien chose for these two peoples funerary traditions that mirror the highly sophisticated but more prescribed rituals of the later Middle Ages and the less ostentatious but more personalized customs of the early Anglo-Saxon period. These practices, laden with their own stories, take on new resonance when moved into a fictional context where they are no longer defunct historical constructs but living traditions. Thus, the burial practices of these two peoples represent the bookends of the period we now call medieval and serve as a framework from which cultural beliefs, fears, and uncertainties can be extrapolated.

Curiously, the burial practices of the hobbits are not depicted in any great detail.[39] Unlike the other cultures of Middle-earth, hobbits' graves are touched on only tangentially and the characters never directly experience them. The only reference to any burials within the boundaries of the Shire comes shortly after the Battle of Bywater, where it is reported that the "ruffians" killed in the battle were hauled off to be buried in an old sandpit, while the fallen hobbits were laid together in a grave on a hillside, later marked by a stone with a garden around it (*RK,* VI, viii, 992). The choice of a hill speaks to Tolkien's predilection for mounds, but it is not quite a mound, and the garden atop it is more reminiscent of the memorial gardens of World War I. In any case, none of the Travellers nor Bilbo—the five hobbits whose graves we were mostly likely to have heard about—ultimately rest in the Shire. Merry and Pippin both die in the South and are interred in Rath Dínen (*LR,* 1072). Sam, Frodo and Bilbo do not die in Middle-earth at all; their eventual deaths in Valinor are not described. So the small take their place among the great and rest in places far grander than they might have—but they give up their homey plot in the garden.

Throughout *The Lord of the Rings,* there is a tacit insistence that the closer an individual is to the earth, the less likely he or she is to fear death.

The hobbits, closest to the earth both literally and metaphorically, display no explicit fear of dying on their quest, though they do fear failure. Aragorn, though the rightful king of Gondor, lives his life wandering the byways of Middle-earth, mingling with its peoples and learning their languages and customs; he is unafraid of both death and the places of the dead. The Rohirrim, too, live close to the natural world, nurturing their beloved horses and working the land they call theirs. Intriguingly, it is the people of Rohan, not of Gondor, who bury their dead in mounds. Since the people of Gondor trace their ancestry to Númenor, it would seem more likely that the descendants of Elros, who have Elvish blood in their veins and once lived in sight of Elvenhome, should follow Elvish burial customs. But it is not so. On deeper reflection, though, the choice makes sense on two levels. First, the fear of death is precisely what caused the Númenoreans to lose their homeland in the first place. Like his ancestors before him, Denethor, who has lived his life in the city, hates and fears death; his suicide in Rath Dínen is an act of defiance rather than acceptance. Second, the Rohirrim of fiction owe a great deal of their culture to the Anglo-Saxons and Goths of history, and Tolkien probably knew more about their languages—and quite a bit more about their cultures—than any other scholar of his day.[40] Since he eventually intended his Legendarium to link up with the "lost" mythology of England, it simply makes sense that he should work Anglo-Saxons' burial customs into his own masterpiece.[41]

The people of Rohan keep their dead firmly in front of them, seeing the places of the dead as continual reminders of history, home, and heritage. In fact, to reach the living city of Edoras, travelers must pass between the graves of the kings: seven mounds lie on the west side of the road, and nine more on the east. The first mound on the west side of the road is Eorl's, the first king of Rohan and the individual who formed the alliance with Gondor; though he died long ago, his memory is continually invoked in both a song sung nightly and the mound passed daily. The sight of the mounds prompts Aragorn to sing "The Lament of the Rohirrim," which simultaneously commemorates and mourns an age forever gone. It has often been noted that the opening lines ("Where now the horse and the rider?" and so on) closely parallel strophe 92 of the Old English *The Wanderer,* a poem of loss for a time that has passed. But whereas the author of

The Wanderer, being Christian, ends by meditating on the steadfastness of the Father in heaven as the only sure comfort, Tolkien's pre-Christian Rohirrim cannot have any such hope.[42] Instead, their ancestors are gone, and their ultimate fate is hidden:

> They have passed like rain on the mountain, like a wind in the meadow;
> The days have gone down in the West behind the hills into shadow.
>
> (*TT,* III, vi, 497)

"The Lament of the Rohirrim" takes the elegiac tone of *The Wanderer* and amplifies it; here there is no wise old man at the end contemplating better things; there is only the sense of transience and loss. Still, hope is not lost. The song and the mounds remain to remind people of what has gone before, and if they cannot be recaptured, at least they need not be forgotten. The mounds thus serve a communal service, confirming the Rohirrim's connection to their land and their history. In the vast history of Middle-earth, the Rohirrim have not really been the Rohirrim very long; Legolas notes that the golden hall of Meduseld was built only five hundred years ago, from the Elvish perspective a very brief period. But Aragorn counters with the observation that to the people or Rohan it seems a long time ago indeed, so long that it is "but a memory of song" (*TT,* III, vi, 496). The mounds act as both physical and metaphysical ties to history.

In real history, too, burial mounds function as ancestral ties to the land; Christopher Daniell and Victoria Thompson, for instance, point out that the placement of the mounds constitutes "an assertive re-creation of the landscape typical of the location of Saxon burial mounds, perhaps announcing ownership of the land," which is effectively "an attempt to identify the new landowner as part of an older tradition."[43] In medieval Sweden and Norway, which were, like Rohan, mostly oral societies, "the mounds built of earth came to be the tangible symbols of the property rights of the families and households in the adjacent settlements."[44] In Iceland, too, mounds "were raised by the family or friends of the deceased, usually near his home in life, and they were always conspicuous features of the local terrain." For instance, barrows of ancestors commonly stood in the household's backyard, confirming the family's relationship to the land in a very visible way.[45]

The placement of the mounds along the road to Edoras is therefore not accidental; it is a deliberate strategy on the part of the rulers of Rohan to confirm their connection to their history and their land.

After his death in the Battle of Pelennor Fields, Théoden too takes his place among the dead Kings of Rohan. His funeral is described in some detail, and although Tolkien certainly drew many details from *Beowulf,* he also used his knowledge of contemporary archaeology to make the scene consistent with what archaeologists of Tolkien's day believed of Anglo-Saxon or Viking funerals. Théoden, for instance, is laid in a stone structure, into which are placed many of his treasures and over which is raised a mound. That the structure was large enough to hold all these things suggests that the mounds were very large indeed—enough, at least, to ensure that it would be noticed by wayfarers along the road to Edoras. Théoden's funeral, too, is commemorated by a song, but this one has a distinctly different effect on its hearers. At Théoden's interment, the Riders "rode round about the barrow and sang together a song of Théoden Thengel's son" (*RK,* VI, vi, 954). Though not everyone present at the funeral can understand the language of Rohan, everyone finds the song moving. But for the people of the Mark, "the words of the song brought a light to the eyes" as they hear again of Théoden's last deeds (954). Whereas the Lament for Boromir feels somewhat detached, as if the name and deeds have simply been filled in, Théoden's threnody is intensely personal, detailing not only what Théoden did but why it was glorious:

> *Out of doubt, out of dark, to the day's rising*
> *he rode singing in the sun, sword unsheathing.*
> *Hope he rekindled, and in hope ended:*
> *over death, over dread, over doom lifted*
> *out of loss, out of life, unto long glory.* (954)

The words of Boromir's funereal song are uncertain, troubling; those of Théoden's are filled with hope. His deeds, and the songs commemorating them, have lifted him over death; he will be remembered. In a society that does not keep written records, the songs and the mounds work together to form the collective memory of a people. Since one of the most important tools for shaping cultural identity is the "commemoration of famous figures who embody the group's ideals and promote a set of common values," it is fitting that the heroes of Rohan should rest in highly visible monuments.[46]

Finally, the funeral ends with a great feast, which also seems to be true of Anglo-Saxon funerals.[47] The feast itself ends with the ritual of drinking from a cup, a clear signal that the Kingship has passed on, and then a listing of the names of the Kings of Rohan. When Théoden is named, Éomer drains his cup; then all stand and drink to the new king, crying, "Hail, Éomer, King of the Mark!" (*RK*, VI, vi, 955).

Although they are collective, not individual, the other mounds in Rohan also serve a commemorative purpose. Four of these lie in the valley outside Helm's Deep and commemorate the great battle that had taken place there. For practical reasons, for most warriors "the battlefield of their last fight is always chosen as their resting place," and Helm's Deep is no exception.[48] Thus there are two mounds in the middles of the field, with the men of the East Dales buried on one side and the men of the Westfold on the other. Still another mound is raised for the fallen Men of Dunland, though this was not widely recognized in English-speaking countries because the line, "But the men of Dunland were set apart in a mound below the Dike" was not included in English editions of the text until 2004.[49]

There is only one other individual who merits individual interment, and he, notably, is not royal: Háma, captain of the King's guard, who fell before the gate at Helm's Deep. While "the work of burial" begins on the battlefield, Théoden stands mourning beside Háma's grave, and "cast the first earth upon his grave" (*TT*, III, viii, 538). Háma's heroism and position might suffice to ensure him an individualized burial, but as Karen Rockow points out, there is no actual evidence that it was a mound—the text says only that he was given his own grave.[50] Patricia Reynolds adds that it would be in keeping with standard Anglo-Saxon burial practices if he were simply laid prone in a grave, over which soil from the grave would be heaped. The "mound" would thus really be only the soil displaced by the body, which will naturally flatten out as the body decomposed, resulting in a flat grave or only a small hump.[51] It may well be that Tolkien intended Háma to have just such a grave, marked with only a single stone such as was made for Snowmane, but there is no textual evidence one way or the other.

For the most part, then, the mounds of Rohan seem to be the burial places of the privileged dead, which would be consistent with prevailing archaeological belief at the time Tolkien was writing. Hilda Davidson shared this perception; she notes that "in Anglo-Saxon times the grave beneath the large impressive grave-mound was not the common lot."[52] The excavation of the great burial mound (Mound 1) at Sutton Hoo, with its vast riches, certainly reinforces the opinion that such conspicuous graves were for the very privileged. Tolkien certainly knew of Sutton Hoo; its re-excavation was very much in the news in the late 1930s, when he began writing *The Lord of the Rings,* and he speaks of the vast treasures contained therein in the commentary accompanying his own translation of *Beowulf.*[53] The belief that only elite members of society merited mounds, however, no longer has the weight of general consensus behind it. New evidence suggests that although the massive mounds like those found at Sutton Hoo or Asthall were probably high-status graves, low mounds, sometimes containing many burials within them, may have been more common than was previously supposed.[54]

But there are exceptions: in later Anglo-Saxon times, barrows were sometimes used specifically for the interment of criminals (see chapter 4), a practice intended to ensure that those who had been evil in this life were tormented in the next. Though the Rohirrim do not seem to carry out this custom, there is at least one troubling barrow within the borders of Rohan: that raised by the Huorns after the Battle of Helm's Deep. While the survivors were busily preparing suitable burials for their own dead, they were troubled by their inability to dispose of the corpses of the Orcs, which were "too great for burial or for burning" (*TT,* III, viii, 532). They move the bodies away from the mounds raised for the Riders who had fallen in battle but are unable to do more than that. Gandalf, who seems to know what will happen, urges them not to worry. During the night, the soldiers hear a great noise, and when the morning comes they find that the wood and the corpses of the Orcs are both gone. Instead, the warriors find a huge pit with stones piled over it, which they believe to be the Orcs' final resting place (539–40). Technically speaking, this is not a mound but a cairn; in any case, it is distinctly different from the other mounds in Rohan: there is neither grass nor flower, nor even complete certainty about who, precisely, lies within. The function of the mound is not that of the cairn: the mounds commemorate the deeds of those interred within and bestow on them a kind of immortality, collectively for the Riders, individually for the kings. The cairn is more or less a place to dump the bodies. Their corpses may be part of the landscape, but they are not part of the land; their enclosure in stone separates them.

So there are at least four mounds at Helm's Deep—and possibly a fifth if Háma's grave, too, is a mound. Théoden and his Riders discover the last mound unexpectedly, as it stands guard over the Fords of Isen. The King and his men had been reluctant to pass that way; the Riders had fought a battle against the forces of Saruman just days before and many of the bodies of the men they had known will be lying there, and none of them wish to see the carrion-beasts ravaging the bodies of so many good and brave Men. But when they reach the river, they find, to their surprise, that a mound has been raised on a small island in the river. Gandalf tells Théoden that he set some of the survivors to this task, ensuring the fallen soldiers an honorable place of rest. Éomer then speaks words that seem almost a ritual blessing: "Here let them rest! . . . And when their spears have rotted and rusted, long still may their mound stand and guard the Fords of Isen" (*TT*, III, viii, 538). The mound thus takes on a special significance. Being hallowed by Éomer's words, it becomes not only a memorial but also an instrument. It gains a purpose, almost a consciousness: it has a duty to provide, as if the dead within retain their ability to serve their country.

The Mounds of Mundburg serve the same purpose. These are only mentioned in a song, an elegy composed after the fact by a bard of Rohan to commemorate the Battle of Pelennor Fields. Their individual placement is not specified, but the men of Gondor and Rohan lie there together. Such a burial is perfectly in keeping with the "long-established conventions of military burial, [that] the graves of ordinary soldiers will go unmarked" while simultaneously expressing the entirely modern belief—arising out of the battlefields of World War I—that every soldier deserved a grave.[55] By burying the men of Gondor and Rohan together, the ties between the two countries are physically and metaphorically strengthened: as the bodies of the fallen decompose, a part of Rohan will come to occupy space in Gondor, an enduring monument to the meaning of promises kept and friendship maintained. The Mounds of Mundburg thus unite the two peoples in a visible and enduring way. Like the mounds at the Fords of Isen and at Helm's Deep, these serve multiple purposes: they are at once monument, marker, and memorial. They mark the place where the battle raged, they stand over the burials more noticeably than any headstone, and they will call to mind the deeds of the men interred within for all who see them.

Not for nothing is it a poet of Rohan that composes the "Song of the Mounds of Mundburg." In Gondor, the pattern breaks: there are no songs to give the stones meaning and history, no laments for the dead. In direct contrast to the Barrowfield—the very sight of which is meant to evoke songs and so renew cultural identity—in Minas Tirith the dead rest in Rath Dínen—the *Silent* Street. Other cultures in Middle-earth may not exactly welcome death, but they do not seek to hide from it—or more accurately, to make it invisible—the way the people of Minas Tirith try to do. And that in itself is ironic, because it is precisely their ancestors' fixation with death and death-denial that put them back in Middle-earth in the first place. The rulers of Gondor build themselves tombs more elaborate than any other found in Middle-earth, and yet they are hidden away from the day-to-day life of the city. Boromir's death is marked by a song without a stone, but the more ordinary pattern in Gondor is stones without songs. The tombs or effigies of the kings give mute testament to the passage of time but do not tell the reader the story of their past.

Despite that, there are three deaths of important Men of Gondor described in *The Lord of the Rings,* Tolkien never allows us to see a standard Gondorian funeral. Boromir's death takes place far from the borders of his land, and his comrades are left to arrange a funeral and burial for him according to their own devices. Denethor's death is likewise plagued by uncertainty and doubt, and Gandalf at least seems to disapprove of his chosen means of disposal. And Aragorn's death, while singularly noble and poignant, is not typical so far as we know. In each of these instances, it is the moment of dying that counts, not necessarily what comes after. Yet Tolkien knew that rituals play an important role in any society, and this last honor the living can give to the dead is both intensely personal and generally cultural.

Though Boromir may be a Man of Gondor, there is no indication that his funeral is typically Gondorian, and the circumstances of his death make it unlikely that his companions could give him one in any case. And yet, aside from Théoden's, the departure of Boromir is the most detailed description of a funeral presented in the entirety of *The Lord of the Rings.*

Having died far from his home in Minas Tirith, the remaining members of the Fellowship almost immediately begin to debate the best means of disposing of his body. Legolas proposes three possibilities: a burial, a mound, and a cairn, none of which are practical under the circumstances (*TT,* II, i, 405). Lacking other options, Aragorn decides on a ship-burial, the only one of its kind in the history of Middle-earth. Tolkien takes his cue from the old Scandinavian custom, which seems to have included laying the body near the mast of the ship and surrounding it with treasures before setting it adrift and possibly afire.[56] Boromir's body is carefully tended and laid in the boat, together with such treasures as he had (the elven-cloak and golden belt of Lórien, his helm, his sword and shield, and the two halves of his horn) along with the spoils of his last battle. Then, the three companions row the funeral boat to the middle of the river and cut it adrift, allowing it to fall over the great fall of Rauros, a clear echo of the departure of Scyld Scefing at the end of the exordium of *Beowulf* or the funeral of Baldr in the *Gylfaginning* (*TT,* III, i, 406–7).

There is no stone at all to mark Boromir's final resting place: he hasn't one. Instead, his companions sing a song to mourn his passing, marking three of the four points of the compass as mnemonics to indicate his uncertain resting place in the wider world. In silence, the three companions watch the boat plunge over the waterfall, and then Aragorn begins to sing:

> *Through Rohan over fen and field where the long grass grows*
> *The West Wind comes walking, and about the walls it goes.*
> *'What news from the West, O wandering wind, do you bring me tonight?*
> *Have you seen Boromir the Tall by moon or by starlight?* (*TT,* III, i, 407)

The song continues for three ten-line stanzas, representing the West, South and North winds. The East wind is omitted, possibly because it would reach Gondor by passing over Mordor. Each verse describes a facet of Boromir's life: his journeys and his final battle. Yet there is something disquieting about these verses, something unresolved. Legolas, who sings the second verse, notes that the South Wind refuses to tell where Boromir has gone, depicting instead a kind of anonymous graveyard where the dead lie together, mingled and nameless:

Ask me not where he doth dwell—so many bones there lie
On the white shores and the dark shores under the stormy sky;
So many have passed down Anduin to find the flowing Sea. (TT, III, i, 408)

The verses Aragorn sings are more optimistic than Legolas's. He sings the last verse, which tells of Boromir's final battle with the Uruk-hai, and the words suggest that Boromir will find forgiveness beyond the sea. Instead of the jumble of anonymous death, he expresses a more individualized fate, where Rauros bears Boromir to a place of rest, though *where* that rest will be is left unsaid (408). It might be that the song refers to the funeral rites enacted by Aragorn, Legolas, and Gimli, or it might refer to a more permanent interment somewhere else. Perhaps these attitudes reflect cultural differences—Aragorn regarding death as the entry to a better world, and Legolas seeing only the empty end of the Elves—but, given the complexity with which Tolkien bestowed his created world, it is possible that the song "existed" before, with the singers only filling in the appropriate names and deeds. Nevertheless, it is clear that Aragorn and Legolas obviously found it appropriate to mark their comrade's passing by singing.

But singing songs for the dead, whether in lament or commemoration or both, does not appear to be the norm in Gondor. The elegy for the dead of the Battle of Pelennor Fields is composed by a bard of Rohan, and while the people of Gondor are perfectly capable of composing beautiful songs of celebration, not once do they sing in memory of the dead. In some ways, the culture of Gondor is defined by the fear of death. In fact, Gondor exists because its forebears' desire to avoid death led directly to the destruction of their island realm; the few survivors took root in Gondor. But even though those Faithful who survived the wreck of Númenor presumably did not share their society's obsession with controlling death—or at least, not enough to prevent them risking their lives to face Sauron—old habits die hard, and the fear of death and the elaborate funereal rituals and buildings linger on in their descendants.

Although Pippin befriends and is befriended by a number of ordinary soldiers, Tolkien does not give them much to say on the subject that so preoccupies the leaders of the City. Like soldiers in real life, they are primarily focused on doing their duties and completing their tasks, and less interested in the political implications of the War. But these ordinary men and women must have put their dead *somewhere*. That alone implies the existence of other cemeteries within the city walls. This practice echoes those found among the ordinary men and women who lived in medieval villages; cemeteries were often the geographical and social center of the community, functioning not only as graveyards but as markets, animal warrens, sanctuaries and trysting-grounds. More elite burials occurred in the church; connected to their communities, perhaps, but separated from their fellow citizens by class and status as well as the more physical barrier of the wall. As Barbara Gusick has pointed out, death is *not* the great leveler: kings get majestic tombs; paupers don't.[57] Even in death, class will tell.

The burial ground of the stewards and the kings is shown through Pippin's eyes, and the experience is frightening and disorienting. Probably because of the Númenorean fear of death, the district of the dead in Minas Tirith is literally relegated to the margins of society. The only entrance lies on the sixth circle of the City, past a great courtyard in which stands a single tree. Beyond it lies a single door in the rearward wall (in other words, up against the flank of the mountain), which is, in turn, guarded by a single porter, a position reminiscent of the watchmen employed to guard medieval cemeteries. No one comes there except those charged with caring for the dead; in contrast to the medieval cemeteries, which were paradoxically bursting with life and activity, the entrance to the Rath Dínen is silent indeed.

The setting is desolate enough, and made more so by the presence of the Withered Tree. In the minds of the Gondorians, the Tree is a sign of the failed line of the Kings who planted it, but they have forgotten or neglected its true significance. The Withered Tree is the last seedling of Nimloth, the white tree that once bloomed in Númenor, which Elendil carried with him when he fled the destruction of the island. Nimloth was the offspring of Galathilion of Valinor, which was the fruit of Telperion, Eldest of Trees (*RK*, VI, v, 950). Although the people of Gondor no longer remember it, the Withered Tree is not a symbol of the *dead* line of kings but a promise of hope and renewal: it is tied back, through many generations, to Elvenhome and the creation of the world, and beyond the world into the eternal realm in which the Valar had their home. The Tree is withered, not dead, and one of its seeds will bloom again. But now it seems almost to weep as Pippin and the rest of the entourage pass: "They

heard the water dripping sadly from the dead branches into the dark water" (iv, 807–8).

Trees and water, of course, are classical signs of impending katabasis,
but here they seem almost actively mourning—whether in grief for Faramir, or in horror of Denethor, or simply for the grief of the world is not
clear. The tree is Pippin's last sight of the upper world before he and his
companions reach the door leading down into the realms of the dead.
The entourage travels continually downward until at last they come to the
Silent Street, Rath Dínen. Though no one lives there, the place seems a
macabre simulacra of the living city above; just as in Minas Tirith, there
are domes and halls. But these houses are silent and not cluttered with
the effluvia of life. The domes are pale, the halls are empty, and in place of
living people there are only "images of men long dead" (RK, VI, iv, 808).
The place is a necropolis, a city built for and by the dead; the living do
not belong there. The living bodies of Pippin, Denethor, Faramir and the
pallbearers are intrusions in the silent stillness of the city of the dead.

At last, the procession reaches the House of the Stewards, and the
guards who have been chosen to carry the suffering Faramir set down their
burden. Pippin looks around and sees the particulars of his environment in
some detail, noting the great sweeping shadows, vast shrouded chamber,
and above all the sleeping forms lying with folded hands and heads pil-
lowed by stone that lay all around him (RK, VI, iv, 808). The image—the
wide vaulted chamber and the praying attitude of the figures—immediately
recalls the great medieval churches and, more specifically, the elaborate
monuments within them. Although Roman monuments were decorated
with images of the deceased, the practice died out near the end of the classical period, only to be revived with remarkable vigor in the twelfth century.
By the thirteenth century, effigies depicting individuals as they were in
life became increasingly popular, though it must be remembered that such
tombs were only for the exceedingly wealthy. For instance, the fifteenth-
century tomb of Richard Beauchamp, Earl of Warwick, was estimated to
cost £720, roughly £497,000 or $800,000 in today's terms. The sheer
extravagance of the tombs made them prohibitively expensive, and by the
end of the seventeenth century the age of the effigies had largely ended,
although vestiges of the practice can still be seen today.

Patricia Reynolds, however, argues that the figures in Rath Dínen "are no effigies, but the embalmed bodies" of the stewards, lying preserved for their descendants' visitations and contemplation. And she may be right; Denethor explicitly forbids the hapless guards under his command to send for the embalmers.[58] Usually, however, if not employed for hygienic purposes, embalming is associated with some sort of belief in an afterlife *for the body,* and such does not appear to be Tolkien's purpose here. Animated corpses do appear in Tolkien's fiction (see chapter 4), but there is no indication that such is the fate Tolkien intended for the stewards, who were presumably generally good (if sometimes misguided) individuals. More likely, it provides further indication that the Gondorians, like their Númenorean ancestors, sought to prevent or delay the onset of death by any means necessary. What can be a clearer denial of the power of death than to halt the most gruesome evidence of its onset, the decomposition of the body?

Simultaneously and paradoxically, the burial practices of Gondor reveal both a deep reverence for the dead and an abiding fear of death. In death as in life, the stewards and the kings clearly believe it necessary to separate themselves from their people—though there is the suggestion that that changes under Aragorn's rule.[59] But there is also the underlying sense that death must not infringe on life; once Fen Hollen has been closed, the past is sealed off, removed from everyday experience. To all intents and purposes, the dead are buried and forgotten, and there is no textual evidence that anybody, regardless of social status, finds this troubling. The existence of the Silent Street permits the living to go on pretending that the dead have been relegated to their place, and that place has nothing to do with the living. To see the dead forces the acknowledgment of death, and in a culture that strives so mightily to separate the dead from the living, the understanding that they have been there all along may be the most frightening realization of all.

With the possible exception of the hobbits, then, the two major human communities portrayed in *The Lord of the Rings* display contrasting attitudes toward the place of the dead. A deep-seated cultural denial of death leads the people of Gondor to create a district of the dead in which the living have no place. Rath Dínen is cut off from the hustle and bustle of everyday life, and the dead are relegated to their places, out of sight and out of mind. In Gondor, the place of the dead is hallowed but avoided; in Rohan, the presence of the dead is simply woven into the fabric of life. To die well is as important as to live well, and while the people of Rohan do not seek death, they accept its presence among them. For the Rohirrim, the graves of the dead are not places to be feared but locations of cultural memory, providing a visible link between the Rohirrim, their history, their heritage, and their homeland. Every traveler journeying to Edoras is placed in the context of the dead, not as a means of intimidation or threat or even a *memento mori,* but simply as an assertion of place, history, and identity. The burial mounds affirm the existence of the ancestors and make the place of the dead the domain of the living. Though death is always present among them, the people of Rohan can live with it.

The memory of the dead defines cultures even as it breaks barriers; traditions may be highly localized and specific, but the experience of grief is universal. In their various ways, the peoples of Middle-earth, like people in the Primary World, cannot quite relegate the past to the past: they must remember those who have died and in so doing give those deaths meaning. For better or worse, we as human beings long to keep our loved ones near. The physical places of the dead, the cemeteries and cenotaphs and the stones we erect there, provide the living with a material connection with the dead. Where there has been great love, those places can offer hope and healing, as Frodo finds at Cerin Amroth. Where there are strong cultural connections, as with the Rohirrim, an entire people can find their national identity. Even great grief, like that of Gimli beside the tomb of Balin, can remind us of our own histories. When no physical places exist, songs and stories can reunite us with the dead, reminding us of who they were and, so, who we have become. In this way, we can assuage the pain of loss and keep the dead in some sense with us. Memory may not be what the heart desires, but in the end, it is all that we have.

CHAPTER 4

Haunting the Dead

The dead have long had a hold on human imagination. Archaeologists maintain that the "awareness of death and our attempts to transcend it have haunted humanity for at least the last ten thousand years and probably the last million years."[1] The archaeological record suggests an almost instinctive need to hallow the dead, to dispose of the remains with dignity, and to ensure that their final places of rest are respected. The same need to ensure that the dead rest in peace also connects with an apparently equally instinctive fear of the dead; they can be sources of malevolence, disease, and danger. As a result, our attitudes toward the places of burial are deeply ambivalent. Even the familiar phrase "Rest in Peace" reflects this ambiguity. On the one hand, it indicates exactly that: a wish that our most beloved departed might indeed rest peacefully in the afterlife, untroubled by the cares and concerns of this world. On the other, however, it means "Stay where we put you and don't come back!"[2]

Just as in the Primary World, the vast majority of the gravesites encountered in Middle-earth are peaceful, serving as symbolic links between the past and the present, the living and the dead. Every so often, however, a grave is not so peaceful, and its societal function as a place of peace and remembrance is disrupted. But these graves, too, are linked to issues of community and immortality, for they are often haunted. Though many "serious" ghost-hunters insist that graveyards are rarely haunted—very few people actually die in a cemetery—popular belief continues to view cemeteries and churchyards as especially haunted locations. Graves represent "fissures in the world through which intimations of immortal damnation can creep," and in cases where communal unease about a death exist—because of a tragedy or a murder, for instance—the dead are particularly likely to rest uneasily or to manifest themselves to the living until their troubles are resolved.[3] The graves of troubled, unusual, or marginalized individuals are particularly susceptible to haunting, and it may be that "adverse circumstances of death may have created 'bad deaths' that required extreme measures often described by archaeologists as 'deviant' burial practices" necessary to keep the unquiet dead in their place.[4]

For the most part, ghosts are associated with sorrow and tragedy, and while they may not always be evil, they are often disturbing. Why some people become ghosts and others rest quietly remains a mystery, but the prevailing view is that something that happened in this world prevents peaceful entry into the next. One popular view is that "ghosts may wander as a punishment to themselves, as in the case of suicides and those who have led evil lives."[5] In his detailed study of the vampire lore of Europe, Paul Barber lists a surprising number of acts that might condemn an individual to an unquiet afterlife, including suicide, murder, death in childbirth, or being conceived during a holy period on the church calendar.[6] In the Middle Ages, ideas of the "good" and "bad" death were often tied up with hauntings: those who had died "bad" deaths, especially deaths that were sudden or violent (and hence did not allow time for repentance), frequently returned as ghosts. Such stories represent a kind of communal unease with the manner of death, particularly in cases where there is a sense that death was too sudden or too violent. Thus, the "ghosts attached to a given locality focus and dramatize, in a particular spot, interpersonal involvements within the whole neighbouring community."[7] Even if individuals are unaware of the historical events, subtle nuances of tone and atmosphere can lead to the impression of supernatural presence; if the individual knows the stories, sightings are even more likely to occur.

The ghosts of Middle-earth echo these beliefs, both medieval and modern. In effect, there are three haunted places in *The Lord of the Rings:* the Barrow Downs, the Paths of the Dead beneath the Dwimorberg and the Mere of Dead Faces in the Dead Marshes. These scenes play on a number of primal fears, including the fear of being buried alive, the fear of trespassing on the places of the dead, and, most of all, the lingering apprehension that some part of our consciousness will remain in the tomb.

The fear of the dead haunts the pages of *The Lord of the Rings* just as it does real life, embodying both medieval and modern anxiety about the dead and the places they inhabit. As with ghosts in the Primary World each of these sites is associated with ancient sorrow and unresolved grief, both for the ghosts and those who witness them. Each of the haunted sites in *The Lord of the Rings* is significant because it explores the boundaries between truth and deceit, faithfulness and faithlessness, courage and cowardice and how each of these influences conceptions of the afterlife. Though *The Lord of the Rings* is a fantasy, its conclusions have very real implications for the dead and the living alike.

The Passage of the Marshes is unique because, more than any other scene in *The Lord of the Rings,* the Mere of Dead Faces reveals Tolkien's complex and subtle blending of medieval folklore and modern experience.[8] On the one hand, the corpse candles that appear to Frodo, Sam, and Gollum are well attested in medieval and modern folklore; they are commonly seen in swamps and marshes and share a long association with the dead. As a medievalist and lover of fairy-stories, Tolkien would have been well aware of these conventions. But the image of dead faces suspended in stagnant water is not found in folklore; it is a direct representation of the real landscape of the Somme. There, the incessant bombing had left the ground pitted and filled with craters into which the bodies of the dead sank. When the rains came, the craters filled with water, so the soldiers passing on wooden walkways overhead looked down into the dead faces of friends and comrades. The image itself is horrifying enough; adding the ghostly lights winking and dancing about the travelers makes the passage of the Marshes thoroughly disquieting. So the imagery of the Marshes owes "something to Northern France after the Battle of the Somme" and something to a long tradition of ghostly lights, blending together to create a scene at once medieval and modern, distinctly unique, and thoroughly horrifying.[9] But though the scene seems to point to the inevitability of death and the wisdom of despair, the underlying message is one that resonates throughout *The Lord of the Rings:* though death may be bitter and the dead should be pitied, the idea that death is cause for despair is only an illusion.

Much of the Marshes' significance is rooted in the history of Middle-earth. Geographically, the Dead Marshes lie on the northwest approach to Mordor, in the space between the Black Gate and the barren hills of

Emyn Muil. Once this territory had been green and fertile, but in year 3434 of the Second Age, the Last Alliance of Men and Elves mounted a great assault on the gates of Mordor (the Morannon). The siege lasted seven years, culminating in the defeat of Sauron and in Isildur's claiming the One Ring as the weregild for his father's death. Afterward, the site of the battle was called the Dagorlad, or "Battle-Plain." In principle, the Last Alliance was victorious, but in effect it only delayed disaster. While not an utter failure, the alliance did not achieve its goals, for though Sauron was defeated, he was not destroyed, and the Ring was "lost but not unmade" (*FR*, II, ii, 237). Worst of all was the terrible slaughter: thousands upon thousands of Elves and Men were killed (238). And while the strength of Elves and Men lessened, Sauron's power slowly took shape and grew again. Millennia later, he returned to his ancient fastness of Barad-dûr and once again planned to destroy the Eldar and their allies. The failures of the first war necessitate the events of the second.

Battlefields, of course, have long histories as haunted places, and graveyards near battlefields are even more notorious. For centuries, people have believed that "certain shades of the dead might remain displaced for some time, particularly the ghosts of those who had died a 'bad death' that was sudden or violent."[10] Since death in battle is violent by definition, war sites are natural breeding ground for ghost stories and sightings. In Britain, reports of ghostly battles abound, ranging from ancient encounters to present-day experiences. For instance, the site of the 1066 Battle of Hastings is haunted by a phantom knight who appears on horseback every October; at the nearby Battle Abbey, a bloody figure believed to be that of the defeated Harold is occasionally seen gazing over the battlefield.[11] A pamphlet published in January 1643, titled *A great wonder under heaven*, describes the Christmas Eve sighting of "ghostly armies fighting through the night," apparently reenacting a battle from the Civil War.[12] The 1746 Battle of Culloden in Scotland was followed almost immediately by stories of shadowy figures seen on the moor; sometimes people report seeing a lone soldier lying as if he's asleep on one of the mounds.[13] In the United States, too, battlefields are often haunted; American Civil War sites in particular seem subject to this phenomenon. The Battle of Gettysburg, the bloodiest of the Civil War, is particularly rich in ghost stories; the History Channel's *Haunted History* devoted two full episodes exclusively to ghosts originating from that battle. Many ghostly regiments are spotted practicing maneuvers—a sight reported only at the locations the of most devastating battlefields, and a strange link between Gettysburg and the Somme, which both have similar reports.

Thus, that Sam, Frodo, and Gollum encounter ghosts as they slowly cross the Dagorlad is not terribly surprising; thousands died and were buried there, and the troubled memory of that battle haunts Middle-earth still. Though the precise location of the graveyard is never stated, it seems to lie on the west end of the battlefield (the same position, coincidentally, occupied by many of the British memorials on the Somme). Another portion of the Dagorlad is only slightly further east, and the narrator mentions that, with a little backtracking, the hobbits might easily have gone that way. However, that route leaves them too exposed; the terrains is so hard and stony that even the cloaks of Lórien could not have hidden them from the watchful eyes of Mordor (*TT,* IV, ii, 611). The safest way tactically is also the most dangerous, for it means that the hobbits must pass through the ancient graveyard.

The way is not pleasant. Frodo gets his first taste of the Marshes well before he sees them: their stink is strong enough to reach the hobbits even in Emyn Muil (*TT,* IV, i, 589). His first glimpse is no more encouraging: reeking mists hover above "dark and noisome pools," stifling the air and obscuring the light. The mountains of Mordor loom in the distance, "a black bar of rugged clouds floating above a dangerous fog-bound sea" (ii, 611). One can hardly imagine a less appealing vista. The half-light and the curling mists immediately suggest haunted places, and the stench of decay only augments that impression. Even its name is ominous; neither "dead" nor "marsh" has a terribly pleasant connotation, and both denote conditions that human beings try to avoid. As the hobbits and their guide penetrate further into the Marshes, they find themselves surrounded by "dead grasses and rotting reeds," and the sun becomes nothing more than "a passing ghost," hardly visible through the thick mists and curling vapors (612). Although any manifestations have yet to be seen, the very air feels haunted and malignant. The whole place is grim and brooding and lends itself to the overall air of foreboding. Once the sun goes down, "the air itself seemed black and heavy to breathe" (613). Shortly thereafter, small, dancing lights begin to appear. These are caused by the release of gasses natural to marshy areas, but their pale blue-green color and unsteady appearance can make even someone who knows what he or she is looking at uneasy. In Tolkien's world, the lights are altogether ominous. They make Sam wonder if he is seeing things and suggest the presence of otherworldly forces.

Cultures throughout the world mention "ghost lights" that appear in a variety of ominous forms, but they are almost always portents of death. In Wales, ancient tradition maintains that when the death of a good person draws near, he or she will receive a warning in the form of a light leading from the home to the burial place, following the funereal route exactly. However, getting in the candle's way could be dangerous or even deadly.[14] In Ireland, corpse-candles are generally borne by those already dead. In Norwegian folklore, ghost lights are associated with the grave-mounds of heroes; in *Njal's Saga,* for instance, the sons of Gunnar come across his barrow and see their father sitting and singing in his mound, with "four lights burning in the mound, and there were no shadows."[15] Occasionally, corpse-candles are even associated specifically with the corpses of fallen soldiers, who arise from their graves with lights in their hands, as is (or was) believed in the Mysore province of Madras in India.[16] In all cases, following the lights is dangerous: they lead travelers astray and frequently to their deaths, where they often light corpse candles in their turn.

Tolkien thus has a long and ominous tradition of ghostly legends behind him, one that will feel hauntingly familiar to readers even if they have no conscious knowledge of the folklore. Thus, when the hobbits find themselves unexpectedly surrounded by the ghostly lights, their apprehension echoes our own. Interestingly, Sam asks Gollum not "*What* are they?" but "*Who* are they?" (emphasis mine), subtly imbuing the lights with purpose and consciousness. But their purpose and consciousness are not reassuring. Gollum explains they are "candles of corpses" and quite sensibly advises that one should neither look at nor follow them, the same advice one would likely receive from any believer in Wales or Ireland or India (*TT,* IV, ii, 613). A few sentences later, Gollum adds a warning not to look into the water when the candles are lit (614). He provides the standard folkloric remedy against corpse-candles: do not pay attention to them, do not follow them, and, above all, *do not interfere* with them. Any attempt to intrude upon the realm of the dead will end badly.

And indeed, that is precisely what happens. Sam, worried about Frodo and anxious about the lights, trips and falls, landing with his face close to the surface of the water. What he sees fills him with a sickened horror. Frodo, too, sees the faces, but instead of reacting with the fear and revulsion we might expect, he replies from an almost trancelike state, his own hands dripping with slime. His response is all the more chilling because it sounds almost more like a chant or an invocation than a description: "I have seen them too. In the pools when the candles were lit. They lie in all the pools, pale faces, deep deep down under the dark water. I saw them: grim faces and evil, and noble faces and sad. Many faces proud and fair, and weeds in their silver hair. But all foul, all rotting, all dead. A fell light is in them." (614) It is the ever-practical Sam who raises the obvious objection: the dead cannot *really* be there. The Battle of Dagorlad took place three thousand years ago; the bodies would have long since decomposed. Frodo's description implies that the faces, for all their foulness, are those of the recently dead: though he says they are rotting (present tense), there is no discoloration (they are fair, instead of black or leathery) or distortion (the faces are grim or noble) commonly associated with the bog people. Furthermore, they do not seem to be there when the candles are *not* lit. All of this is deeply ambiguous and raises the question of whether or not the faces in the Mere are actually present, or only illusions.

Gollum provides the critical clue. He reveals that the faces are incorporeal; he tried to reach them once but could not, which hints that the dead cannot be material remains (*TT,* IV, ii, 614). He then complicates the matter even further. The faces in the Mere, he says, belong to the warriors who fought and died in the Battle of Dagorlad long ago; the marshy ground around them in fact was once a battlefield. The marshes have grown and "swallowed up the graves" in the intervening millennia (614). In seeking to finish the tasks left undone, Frodo must follow in the footsteps of the ancient warriors as he travels to Mordor in his turn. Like them, he must cross the space between the Emyn Muil and the Morannon, and to do so he must walk on their graves.

Ultimately, the real horror of Frodo's vision lies in this confused tangle of the dead. Any distinct graves that the deceased might have occupied have long since disintegrated, absorbed in a creeping flood that honors no boundaries, not even the line between the living and the dead. It is a grim foreshadowing of the fate that lies at the end of the road for all of us. Even worse is the sense that the dead did nothing to deserve this fate; the Elves and Men submerged in the Mere were not particularly cruel or evil, but they lie mingled with the Orcs just the same. The ruthless jumble of the dead suggests that being good results in no better an end than being bad. Everyone, whether Elf or Orc, evil or noble, is "reduced to weeds and foulness in the end."[17] Any resistance to evil is futile and will not really make any difference in the end: the dead are all dead alike.

But, as Sam insists, the dead cannot really be there. The "fell light" emanating from the dead bodies immediately raises the suspicion that supernatural forces are at work, and moreover that those forces are not benevolent. Like the corpse candles that signal their presence, the bodies in the Mere illuminate nothing; it is light "robbed of its simple natural function," just as the bodies trapped in the Mere have been robbed of their natural ability to decompose.[18] In all likelihood, Sam's suggestion that the presence of the dead is only some trick of Sauron's is probably the right one (*TT*, IV, ii, 614). In *The Hobbit*, Sauron is called "the Necromancer." And what do necromancers do but use their magic to manipulate the dead? Since any potential invaders of Mordor would almost certainly have to cross through the Marshes, this horrifying illusion serves as a gruesome deterrent, a psychological barrier in addition to the physical one.

The final power of the Dead Marshes, then, lies not in its horrible visions or seductive lights but in its powerful enticement to give up, to set aside the will to resist evil. If, as Margaret Sinex has argued, the real danger of the corpse candles is to "symbolize the temptation of suicide for the Ringbearer," it also makes his perseverance "more poignant and laudable."[19] It is easy to give up, and tempting to believe that nothing one says or does will make any difference whatsoever: we will all end up dead anyway. If the intent of Sauron's grotesquely illumined corpses is to drain hope, it succeeds; but if it is meant to emphasize the futility of attacking him, it fails. As is the case with the images shown to Denethor in the *palantír*, the faces in the Dead Marshes distort the truth. Frodo and Sam have already accepted that the completion of their quest will almost certainly result in their deaths, and they determined to carry on anyway—a decision that will lead, eventually, to Sauron's destruction (*TT*, IV, ii,

610). Resisting evil, then, is not really futile at all: this is only an illusion, just like the corpse candles and the faces in the Mere. The persistent courage of Frodo and Sam, so quiet that it is often overlooked, is ultimately what allows them to defeat the Marshes.

It is a mark of the tragedy of war that all three sets of ghosts in *The Lord of the Rings* arise directly from the long conflict with Sauron. Two of the three date from the days of the Dagorlad, the great battle that ended the Second Age. But while the dead in the Mere may be wholly illusory, unfortunate victims of Sauron's sorcery, the Dead that haunt the passes under the Dwimorberg have a form and substance all their own. Théoden reports to Merry the long legends of "Dead Men out of the Dark Years" who may occasionally be seen "passing out of the door [under the Mountain] like shadows." When this happens, "the people of Harrowdale shut fast their doors and shroud their windows and are afraid. But the Dead come seldom forth and only at times of great unquiet at coming death" (*RK,* V, iii, 780). In a few sentences, so simply and directly that it often passes unnoticed, Tolkien combines a variety of medieval traditions regarding the dead and their existence in the afterlife, most notably the purgatorial punishment of transgressors lingering after death.

The dead have long served as harbingers of death. Such a belief makes, after all, a certain kind of sense: the best and most appropriate time for an individual to see the dead is when death itself is approaching. Medieval *exempla* and *miracula* are filled with stories of the dead returning to warn the living of their own approaching deaths, and the early Middle Ages in particular tended to depict such visitations as almost reassuring. In book 4 of the *Ecclesiastical History of the English People,* for instance, the Venerable Bede reports a number of instances of the dead returning to assure their brothers and sisters that they are soon to be welcomed to the celestial courts.[20] Usually, though, these individuals have been granted a divine dispensation. Throughout the early half of the Middle Ages, the church officially and repeatedly denied the existence of ghosts, but slowly, the persistence of such stories—coupled with the realization that there was money to be made—led to the official incorporation, if not acceptance, of such beliefs. The most influential of these late medieval texts was Caesarius of Heisterbach's *Dialogue on Miracles* (1223), which routinely shows the recently deceased appearing to their distraught friends or relatives, frequently with the suggestion that a small donation to the church would ease the visitant's own eventual entry into the afterlife. Since the *Dialogue on Miracles* is one of "the primary sources of *exempla* [intended] to pad sermons addressed to laypeople and no longer just to monks" its pages lend a great deal of insight into the relationship between official teachings and popular belief.[21] The return of the dead was most often comforting and peaceful, relatively free from fear and certainly transfused with faith.

But in the popular imagination, as far as we can tell, the return of the dead was often anything but comforting. These reports, too, were almost always written by clergy, but these men were more removed from the theological debates of their era and more closely connected with the lives of everyday people. Far from delivering comforting messages about peace and happiness in the afterlife, their stories often concern the unquiet dead—although the authors see no reason not to add a religious resolution when possible. In *De nugis curialium* (circa 1190), Walter Map tells of a corpse that emerged from its grave to wander the streets of Hereford at night, calling out the names of people who subsequently sickened and died. It was finally conjured into its grave when the bishop wrote it a writ of absolution.[22] Another author, William of Newburgh, reports four incidents of haunting where the restless dead had the unfortunate habit of terrorizing the living.[23] Though a debate was already raging inside the church—were these creatures the animate bodies of human beings, or demonic apparitions sent by Satan to deceive the living?—in Newburgh's accounts the ghosts are consistently described as "ill-intentioned from their own desires or instinct" and not "animated by the Devil for the downfall of the human race."[24] In other accounts, the stories are almost comical. An anonymous monk of Byland Abbey, for instance, tells of one particularly unfortunate revenant that was attacked by a pair of juveniles as it rose from its grave and pinned to the church stile before one of the boys ran for the village priest. The priest absolved the ghost's sins, after which it did, in fact, rest in peace.[25]

In Iceland, however, the restless dead receive the most attention; the idea of an ill-intentioned ghost begetting more ghosts is frequently found in the Icelandic sagas. The most obvious example is the late fourteenth-century *Eyrbyggja Saga,* which sometimes feels as if the anonymous author "deliberately sought out as many as possible of the vague and shadowy beliefs about the dead" as he could integrate into one story.[26] Usually, a *draugr* was malevolent to begin with; death had simply removed the consequences that such behavior would have produced while alive. As a result, the reappearance of one dead person frequently signals the impending death of not just one individual, but several, as if the malicious ghost could not be satisfied with merely extracting revenge on those who "deserved" it. Probably the most famous of these hauntings is that of the *draugr* Thorolf, who "was so malignant that it killed people and others had to run for their lives" (314). He is only stopped when Thorodd, an important farmer, disinters his corpse and burns it to ashes; the ashes infect a bull, which then becomes so malicious that nobody can approach it, until at last the bull runs into a swamp and drowns. At Kjartan's farmstead, the death of a shepherd triggers a cascade of ghosts, ending only when the living bring a lawsuit against the dead for trespassing. In still another instance, a shepherd called Freystein sees a severed human head chanting a verse predicting an impending battle; this is deemed, with typical Scandinavian understatement, "very ominous."[27] To no one's surprise, Freystein's friend Egil is killed a few days later.

Throughout Northern Europe, there was a strong belief that seeing someone already dead indicated one's own looming death—or, at the very least, was indicative of an impending disaster. Throughout the literature of the Middle Ages, the appearance of ghosts is frequently "connected with tumult and change, for great events (battles, plagues, revolts) are announced by forerunners and apparitions."[28] To see the dead is to recognize one's own death. Small wonder that the people of Harrowdale prefer to shroud their windows instead of themselves.

In the *exempla* and in folklore, life and death are linked: one's deeds in this life foretell one's fate in the next. If one has been a good individual and died a good death, one will go on to the final reward, but those who have failed and sinned will be punished in this world as well as the next one. Gradually, the stories of the restless dead met and fused with other traditions, linking the idea of a troop of the damned with the idea of punishment for sins committed while on earth. A story recorded by Peter the Venerable (circa 1092–1152), Abbot of Cluny, tells of the ghost of an old servant who haunts his former master, Pedro d'Englebert. In this account, the servant suddenly appears to Pedro, sitting next to the fire and turning over coals. The servant is naked except for a loincloth, and when challenged, he outlines his reasons for being there: "I am going to

Castile, and a great army is travelling along the same road as me so that we might be free of the punishment incurred by our sins, in the very place where we committed them."[29] Shortly after, he asks that Pedro's wife pay the remainder of his wages, some eight sous, over to the church.

The idea of a great army doomed to perpetually wander the earth in punishment for some sin is widespread and appears in many texts. The story almost certainly has roots in folklore and perhaps derives "from the popular concept of the pagan god Wotan as a wandering huntsman." One of the most famous of these accounts is the encounter between the priest Walchelin and Hellequin's Hunt, recounted in Orderic Vitalis's *Historica Ecclesiastica* (circa 1115–33). Very briefly, the priest Walchelin is traveling home alone on the night of January 1, 1091, when suddenly he hears "the kind of sound made by the passage of a great army." Barred from hiding in a nearby group of medlar trees by a giant, he stands and watches as the procession files past. First, he sees a large crowd on foot, many of whom Walchelin recognizes as local villagers who had died recently. Next comes a group of people enduring torture; murderers tied to biers enduring repeated lashings, and women being pierced with red-hot nails. These are followed by a group of monks, followed in turn by a group of knights. Again, Walchelin recognizes some of them, and one of them addresses him, begging him to convey a message to the dead knight's wife, but the other dead intervene. Gradually, it occurs to Walchelin that he is seeing Herlequin's Hunt, but decides no one will believe him unless he has some proof. He grabs the bridle of a jet-black horse, at which point a troop of knights in black armor threaten him. For his attempted theft, the knights intend to make him join the hunt, and they probably would have succeeded but for the intervention of William of Glos, who wants Walchelin to take a message to his family. Walchelin, who seems not to have been over-endowed with common sense, refuses; the knight seizes the priest by the throat, but he is spared through the intervention of Walchelin's brother Robert. The brother implores the priest to pray for him and to mend his ways, then hastens on. Walchelin returns home gravely ill, and though he recovers, he bears the handprint of William of Glos around his throat for the rest of his life.[30]

Orderic records a Christianized version of a much older story, itself the fusion of still older stories. Even in the folkloric accounts, Herlequin's

Hunt (also called Hellequin's Hunt, or King Herla's Hunt) is not without its penal element. According to the story, the ancient King Herla makes an ill-advised pact with the king of the dwarfs, a term that is sometimes a euphemism for the dead.[31] In most versions of the story, Herla visits the underground realm, but when it comes time to leave, the dwarf king loads him and his entourage down with gifts, including a bloodhound. But, as is almost always the case when dealing with dwarfs, there is a consequence: Herla and those with him must not dismount before the dog does; if they do, they will crumble into dust. From that day forward, Herla and his Hunt are condemned to ride forever, because the dog will never dismount.

The other legend is that of the Wild Hunt, in which the quarry is often a human figure. The *Petersborough Chronicle* reports a sighting in 1127; like the troop seen by Walchelin, the riders are described as *swarte 7 micele 7 ladlice*, "black & great & loathly"; their mounts and hounds are described in similar terms.[32] A number of sources seem to believe the hunters were demons and their quarry was human souls; others maintain they were "either demons pursuing dead sinners, or damned souls themselves."[33] In any case, a sighting of the Wild Hunt signaled impending calamity. The Norwegian variant, the *oskorei*, stops at places where a murder has been or will be committed, while in England the Wild Hunt was commonly viewed as an omen of disaster.[34] Walter Map, however, thought the riders were, like King Herla himself, under an evil enchantment and could not rest or stop, and we must be careful not to "confuse the Wild Hunts with those of the cursed huntsmen."[35]

Characteristically, Tolkien's mythology blends these opposing traditions, creating a version of the Hunt that is demonized but not demonic, unredeemed but not unredeemable. That Tolkien was aware of such a legend is evident in the language he uses to describe the journey of the Oathbreakers. When Aragorn and the Grey Company emerge from beneath the Haunted Mountain, they ride madly toward the Stone of Erech. Though Aragorn and his followers have no intention of harming anyone, the people who live in the valley between the mountain and the stone cry out in terror and run "like hunted deer," and although it pursues a different quarry, the Grey Company rides "like hunters" (*RK*, V, ii, 771). The people of the valley cry out "The King of the Dead!" as the Company rides past, though it is not clear of whom they speak. Most likely, it is the ancient

King who betrayed his oath, but they could be referring to Aragorn.[36] In this moment, Aragorn's identity has been conflated with Herla's; for the Dead are constrained to follow him, forced by the power of an ancient curse to obey the one who has summoned them to the Stone of Erech. For a time, Aragorn commands the Dead.

For Aragorn alone has the power to free the Oathbreakers from their long haunting beneath the mountain. Once, long ago, these Men of the Mountain were warriors who swore to Isildur that they would ride to battle with him when he and his allies went to war with Sauron. But when the time came, they did not fulfill their pledge because they had once worshiped Sauron. Aragorn explains both the curse and the prophecy: summoning the Oathbreakers to the Stone of Erech, Isildur told their king that he would be the last, and that they could not rest in peace until their oath was fulfilled (*RK*, V, ii, 764–65). Like the hapless riders in Herlequin's Hunt, the Shadow Host bears the consequences of their betrayal even after death. As a general rule, even modern readers understand the importance of keeping a promise, although failure to do so may not carry the weight it once did. But in the medieval tradition in which *The Lord of the Rings* is steeped, oath-taking and -breaking were more than just social conventions; they were the bonds that held an oral-based society together. Literature throughout the Middle Ages emphasizes the importance of keeping one's word, even at great personal cost. In texts such as *Beowulf* and the *Völsungsága,* the heroic oath means "the hero is duty bound to fight the dragon or die in the attempt, and his only concern is to do it well."[37] The reason so much stress is laid upon the importance of keeping an oath is simple enough: without, it society would collapse:

> Why is the theme of word as bond so central to the conflicts of so much major English feudal literature? Because it is a master trope, a master figure by which feudal society defined itself. . . . As society centralized, fealty also became centralized, attached to the person of the king. It is important to realize that this fealty was a personal affair, a bond between persons, modeled on the bond between fathers and sons and uttered as a word—an oath of allegiance. . . . Therefore, feudal literature, carrying out its encoding function, focuses repeatedly on the defining thesis of society, word as bond, and its antithesis, the ultimate transgression—betrayal.[38]

The dangers of oath-breaking even appear in the famous *Sermo Lupi ad Anglos,* given by the Archbishop Wulfstan of Ely in 1014. One thousand years later, we are used to finding the idea of keeping one's word emphasized in secular sources, but "finding those elements in a sermon, the genre whose job it is to apply the gospel to everyday life, suggests that, to the Old English mind, or at least to Wulfstan's eleventh-century Old English mind, the making (and breaking) of oaths is an everyday moral concern not limited to the heroic age."[39] Wulfstan lists oath-breaking among the many sins committed by the English, ranking it as deadly as murder, kin slaughter, and avarice: *Ne ænig wið operne getrywlice þohte swa rihte swa he scolde, ac mæst ælc swicode and oþrum derede wordes and dæde*—"Nor has anyone thought loyally toward the other as justly as he should, but almost all have been treacherous and have betrayed others by words and by deeds."[40] Wulfstan also uses the word *āðbrice* in this sermon, a *hapax legemon* that appears nowhere else in the extant Old English corpus but translates as "oath breach" or "oath break."

The same idea is stressed in *The Battle of Maldon*. Although Tolkien regarded the primary fault as Beorthnoth's, contemporaries viewed the men who fled the field as thoroughly contemptible. Upon seeing them leave, the first reaction of the remaining warriors is outright disbelief that the deserters could so easily dishonor their former pledges. Ælfwine, the first to speak, says in almost palpable horror:

> Gemunu þā mæla þe we oft æt meodo spræcan
> þonne we on bence bēot āhōfon,
> Hæleð on healle, ymbe heard gewinn;
> nū mæg cunnian hwā cēne sy (ll. 212–15)

["Remember the occasions when we often said at mead, when we on the benches lifted up boasts, the hero in the hall, about hard battle; now we may find out who is keen."]

Ælfwine's words inspire the other members of the *heorðwerod*—the hearth-companions, the most trusted warriors—not only to remember their oaths but to repeat them; Leofsunu, for instance, answers Ælfwine by affirming *"Ic þæt gehāte, þæt ic heonon nelle / flēon fōtes trym"* (ll. 246–47a; "I swear this, that I will not flee the space of a foot"); the others all utter similar vows.[41] Even the humble peasant Dunnere, who might presumably be excused from such a heroic undertaking, asserts his loyalty to his fallen leader by refusing to leave the battle. There are a number of good reasons why a warrior might have felt justified in suddenly remembering pressing duties elsewhere, not least of which was a king who was in the process of becoming a "national symbol for English unwillingness to stand and fight." But the poem makes clear that for the most part, leaving the field was an almost unimaginable sin. It could earn punishment in the next life, associated as it was with the ultimate traitor, Satan himself. After all, his primary sin in the eyes of the Anglo-Saxons was disloyalty.[42] If the soul of a good man like Beorthnoth could be in jeopardy for one horrible mistake, what would be the penalty for someone who broke society's most deeply entrenched code? Though the eventual deaths of the Oathbreakers is not discussed in *The Battle of Maldon,* the implication in the poem is that their lot will not be a happy one. From history, we know it was not.

Even after the Anglo-Saxon period was over, the belief that people who broke their vows were forced to linger in a shadow-state until their oaths were fulfilled lingered through the centuries. In Ulster, for instance, people believed until recently that "wilful or unintentional neglect of even minor promises and duties while living may cause a ghost to appear after death."[43] A Danish collection called the *Dansk Sagn,* compiled by Evald Tang Kristensen in the late nineteenth century, also links the act of breaking one's word to an otherworldly punishment:

> In heathen times the Oath-Takers ("Sandemaend") ere like a court. When people went to them and swore on their word, it was taken to be the absolute truth. When they divided the fields "the men" (i.e., owners of farms) of Stjarr village put leaves from their own trees in their hats and earth from their own land in their clogs, and swore that what they stood on and what the stood under was their own, and might they turn into grey stones if they swore falsely. And that is what happened to them on the way home.[44]

The Stone of Erech, too, maintains this association with the oath-breaking Dead; it functions not as a marker for mortal remains but as a memorial to a broken promise. Therefore, Aragorn summons them to precisely the place where their oath was broken and their curse was cast when he begins the process of reversal: if they help him free Pelargir from the forces of Sauron, he will hold their oath fulfilled, and allow them to finally die (*RK*, V, ii, 772). Aragorn is able to command the allegiance of the Shadows not simply because he is going to war against Sauron but because he is going to war against Sauron as Isildur's heir. Just before taking the Paths of the Dead, Aragorn chose to reveal his existence to Sauron through the *palantír* serendipitously recovered from Isengard. Undoubtedly, he made this move for precisely the reasons he says he does: to make Sauron uncertain, and therefore risk a strike before his army is fully prepared. But it also establishes the war as a clash between Aragorn and Sauron, a necessary confrontation if his claim that he leads the Dead into battle against Sauron is to be recognized by the Dead. Once he has cemented the ties between his blood and the resistance to Sauron's domination, he can claim to lead even the Dead, because "death does not end vassalic obligations."[45] The Dead are his to command.

And they are, in their final battle, extremely effective. Though Legolas says he thought they were only "the shadows of Men, powerless and frail," they are corporeal enough to aid Aragorn in the fight (*RK*, V, ix, 856). They sweep over the forces of Sauron at Pelargir. Gimli, who tells the tale, says he does not know if their weapons are still effective, but he can hear them calling and blowing their horns (858). His account of the battle does not answer the question of the corporeality of the Dead, but it does not doubt their effect: they are terrifying, as terrifying as encountering the Wild Hunt. Here, too, the "dim horns blowing" and the "murmur of countless voices" echo the rushing wind of medieval folklore. But, unlike the Wild Hunt, this phantom army has the hope of peace. Once Pelargir is freed, Aragorn releases them (858). As soon as he does so, "the King of the Dead stood out before the host and broke his spear and cast it down. Then he bowed and turned away; and swiftly the whole grey host drew on and vanished like a mist" (859). Breaking the weapons of war that bound them to earth becomes a symbolic act: a betrayal of a war-oath bound them to the world, but the fulfillment of the same oath releases them from it. Wherever the Shadow Host goes, they no longer trouble the living, and they are never encountered in Middle-earth again. The Dead, having atoned for their crime and completed their tasks, can finally rest in peace.

Thus, the Haunted Mountain is haunted no more, and the Mere of Dead Faces was probably never really haunted in the first place. The Barrow-downs, however, are altogether different. Barrows have a long history as haunted places. This association makes, after all, a certain kind of sense: since the physical remains of the dead linger in the place of burial, so must the spiritual. As Theo Brown observes, "when educated men toyed with the notion that the earth in a burial ground was saturated with the virtue of dead corpses, it is hardly surprising that ordinary folk reckoned such places to be haunted."[46] Given the dramatic scale of the structure, it could well be that the function of creating a barrow—or, for that matter, any kind of organized burial place—is to link "the past with the present, and the living with the dead and the supernatural."[47] Although almost any burial site might give rise to an attendant ghost story, barrows seem to attract more than their fair share. Moreover, barrows in particular tend to house the malevolent dead. Some scholars believe barrows were preferentially used for the interment of criminals, potentially because the officials wished them to be tormented in the afterlife by the evil spirits that dwelled in the mound.[48] This, then, is the foundation upon which Tolkien's barrow is built: the abode of the dangerous dead, of dragons and demons and other things dark and dangerous.

In the Icelandic sagas, the *draugr* or *haugbúi* are barrow-dwellers. Though the saga-writers used the two terms somewhat interchangeably, most modern scholars agree that the *draugr* wanders farther from its barrow and is driven by some strong emotional impetus, such as greed, revenge, or even homesickness. The *haugbúi* (lit. *haug* ę "howe, cairn"; *bú* = "household") tends to be a homebody and does not readily leave its barrow, and it sometimes becomes "miserly about its grave-goods and reluctant to fight the barrow-breaker who would deprive it of even this shadow life."[49] Because they are undoubtedly linked to specific barrows and do not seem to wander about, the term *haugbúi* seems more appropriate when speaking of the wights, but either term certainly has its place on the barrow-wight family tree. In fact, a widely distributed Internet article describes the entire barrow scene: "In modern times, the most familiar encounter with a *draugr* is Frodo's spectral struggle with the 'barrow-wight' in J. R. R. Tolkien's book *The Fellowship of the Ring,* in the chapter 'Fog on the Barrow-Downs.'" Though there are some difficulties with this rather glib definition, there is little doubt that Tolkien's barrow-wight is kin to the Old Norse ghosts.

The *haugbúi* and the barrow-wight share a number of common traits, most obviously that they both dwell in barrows. They are not disembodied ghosts but revenants, walking corpses that threaten the living and must be defeated by a human hero. But there are other, more subtle variations of the *haugbúi* present in the wight. Both have preternaturally glowing eyes; the sight of the moonlight reflected in the revenant Glam's eyes, for example, gives the hero Grettir an unshakeable fear of the dark thereafter. Similarly, just before he is captured by the barrow-wight, Frodo thinks he sees eyes lit with a pale, cold light that somehow seems to come from far away (*FR*, I, viii, 136). Both can use fell magic; Agnar's barrow, for instance, is said to be protected with witchcraft, a kind of magic with distinctly negative connotations, similar to the "dreadful spells of the Barrow-wights" that Frodo fears (137).

One of the most unexpected and distinctive traits of the *haugbúi* shared by the barrow-wight is its strong association with *skaldscip*, with music and poetry. A number of Norse texts mention the barrow-dweller's ability to grant the gift of eloquence to those brave—or foolish—enough to sleep on its barrow. Admittedly, variations of this idea appear in other cultures as well; Chris Barber, for instance, reports in *Mysterious Wales* that anyone sitting on Idril's Seat is liable to end up "a corpse, a madman or a brilliant poet."[50] But in the Norse tradition, it is clear that "the association of poetry is primarily with the dead, rather than with their burial place."[51] In many instances, the *haugbúi* is reported as singing in its grave, just as the barrow-wight does. In *Njal's Saga,* for instance, Gunnar's sons report seeing an image of their father in his burial mound, reciting a verse "so loudly that they could hear it, even at a distance."[52] The wight also sings in its barrow; shortly after awakening there, Frodo hears a song, a "formless stream of sad but horrible sounds" which every now and again form words (*FR*, I, viii, 137). Frodo quickly realizes, to his horror, that the words have become an incantation which seems to doom the listener to a cold, hard existence between life and death:

Cold be hand and heart and bone,
and cold be sleep under stone:

never more to wake on stony bed,
never, till the Sun fails and the Moon is dead.
In the black wind the stars shall die,
and still on gold here let them lie,
till the dark lord lifts his hand
over dead sea and withered land. (137)

Part of the terror of this scene, of course, lies in the universal fear of waking up to find oneself imprisoned in a tomb. Even worse is waking up to find that the earlier inhabitant has not quite left it and does not want company. Both embody the ancient fear that one's death does not automatically grant entrance to the afterlife, or worse yet, that this *is* the afterlife and one is doomed to remain, conscious but immobilized, trapped in a decaying body but with a full comprehension of what is going on. Both the Old Norse and Anglo-Saxon traditions speak to this fear, and the texts take a variety of forms, from folklore to sermons to sagas, that suggest "a widespread belief that the soul, periodically at least, could be closely linked with the body."[53] In the Anglo-Saxon tradition, the most obvious examples are the *Soul and Body* poems, in which the Soul returns every seventh night to visit the decaying and helpless body it once inhabited. *Soul and Body I,* found in the Vercelli Book, shows the Soul returning to harangue its body for the sins it committed in life, sins that now have condemned it to "the place where people live in disgrace," while in the Exeter manuscript's *Soul and Body II,* the soul lives in the bliss of heaven—but both return. Wright cites a less well-known example, noting a text with Celtic connections from Corpus Christi College, Cambridge, MS 279, which claims that after death the soul visits four sites significant in its life: the place where it died, its grave, its birthplace and the site of its baptism. Furthermore, the text states that the soul returns to the grave of its body every Sunday; where it "feels (and presumably expresses) loathing (*tedium*) toward the body."[54] In the most horrific cases, the soul apparently has never left the body at all, and the animated remains return to threaten the living.

Such is the situation in which Frodo finds himself. He recognizes almost immediately that he has awakened in a barrow, a liminal space between the realm of the living and dead. Instead of the proverbial quiet of the tomb, he hears a "creaking and scraping sound" and turns to see a long arm, groping, walking on its fingers toward Sam, Merry and Pippin, who are lying with a naked sword across their necks. After a moment's hesitation, Frodo leaps up, seizes a convenient sword, and hacks off the hand, but doing so causes the sword to break right up to the hilt. Simultaneously, something shrieks, the light goes out, and in the sudden darkness something begins to snarl (*FR*, I, viii, 138). It is not a comforting moment.

That, too, plays on a feature of the *haugbúi:* it can only be slain by its own sword and only by a hero. In fact, the usual method of defeating a *haugbúi* was decapitation, a feat Frodo does not achieve, though he does maim the wight with a sword from its own barrow. But Frodo follows heroic action with poetic action: he chants the verse that brings Tom Bombadil to the hobbits' aid. In Tolkien's version, the encounter with the barrow-wight does not grant the gift of eloquence—Frodo never becomes a very good poet—but Frodo's verse nevertheless summons Tom Bombadil, and Bombadil banishes the wight with a song.

And finally, there is all that treasure. Although archaeologists are quick to point out that treasure-laden barrows are actually very rare, people continue to believe most barrows are positively bursting with gold.[55] There are plenty of examples of *haugbúar* jealously guarding their treasure. For example, in "The Tale of the Cairn-Dweller," a man called Thorstein is confronted by the ghost of the man whose sword he has stolen; and the cairn-dweller demands—in verse, no less—that the sword be returned.[56] Unlike the *haugbúi* of tradition, however, there is simply no direct evidence that the barrow-wight of *The Lord of the Rings* cares all that much about its treasure, although it has it in abundance. The barrow-wight's tomb is filled with riches: Frodo sees his three friends lying as if asleep on heaps of treasure and adorned with gold, and after the barrow-wight's defeat, Bombadil emerges carrying armfuls, some of which are as full of historical significance for the hobbits as the artifacts of Sutton Hoo are to us.

The idea of treasure in a barrow, though, almost automatically brings up another creature, arguably the most famous barrow-dweller of them all: the dragon of *Beowulf.* Like the wight, he is the possessor of riches in abundance, and, like the wight, the treasure he guards is probably not rightfully his. Since the wight is described in specifically human terms—it has hands and fingers, not claws, and there is no mention of the scales or fire associated with dragons elsewhere in Tolkien's fiction—Patrick Callahan's straightforward assessment that "the barrow-wight resembles Beowulf's dragon" seems as oversimplified as the internet article's assertion that the barrow-wight is a *draugr*—but the dragon probably also deserves a branch on the barrow-wight's family tree.[57] For one thing, several scholars have pointed out that the dragon in *Beowulf* acts like a *draugr*: it dwells in a barrow, it jealously guards its treasure, and it is a distinct threat to the living. Moreover, there is certainly a connection "between the dragon who so resents interference with his treasure and the dead man himself."[58] In fact, several scholars have considered the possibility that the dead man himself became the dragon. The idea that a man could become a dragon may seem extraordinary to us, but there are precedents. In *The Saga of the Volsungs*, for instance, Fafnir turns into a dragon after attaining the dwarf Andvari's treasure; another Old Norse tale, "Gull-thorir's Saga" tells of an extremely odd family of dragons who were once men; after their transformation into dragons, they sleep on chests of gold.[59] The end of the saga returns to the same theme, with speculation that Gull-thorir himself might have been transformed into a dragon.[60]

In medieval art, the dragon is also associated with demons, sometimes with Satan himself. Because the Anglo-Saxons converted to Christianity long before the Scandinavians, it is not surprising that a number of their barrow-dwellers receive a more obviously Christian interpretation. Since barrows were raised predominantly over pagan dead, these barrows acquired more demonic overtones as the new religion took hold. Probably the most obvious literary example of this is the story of the seventh-century saint Guthlac, who goes into the wilderness and takes up residence in a *beorg*, a mound or barrow. Whatever the historical Guthlac's experience may have been, both *Guthlac A* and *B* record that he found the place already inhabited by demons. This interpretation is unique to the Anglo-Saxon version of the story; the Latin source (Felix's *Vita Sancti Guthlaci*) places the battle with the demons in the wilds *outside* the barrow, not within it, suggesting a shift in the perception of barrows and their inhabitants, on the part of the two writers at the very least.[61] The demons, who use the barrow as their entry into this world, naturally resent Guthlac's coming and do all they can to drive him out. Only after enormous effort is Guthlac able to banish them. The barrow becomes a battle-ground, just as it does for Frodo, and ultimately the *sigewong*, the "field of victory" for both heroes.

The Wife's Lament suggests another potential account of condemned spirits haunting their graves. Old English poems are notoriously difficult to translate into modern English; the syntax, punctuation, and modes of expression are very different. Furthermore, several words can carry several layers of meaning at once, layers that no longer appear in modern English and thus make it difficult for a translator to convey the same meaning as the original. In particular, the slippage in the words used to describe the narrator's place of confinement has led some scholars to read *The Wife's Lament* as a ghost story. I have boldfaced the words that allow the most significant change in meaning.

Forþon is min hyge geomor,
ða ic me ful gemæcne   monnan funde,
heardsæligne,   hygegomorne,
mod miþende,   **morþor** hycgendne.
Bliþe gebæro   ful oft wit beotedan
þæt unc ne gedælde   nemne deað ana
owiht elles;   **eft** is þæt onhworfen,
is nu   swa hit no wære
freonscipe uncer.

. . . .

Heht mec mon wunian on wuda bearwe,
under actreo   in þam **eorðscræfe**. (ll. 17–25, 27–28)[62]

Following the convention of leaving in the editors' punctuation intact, this passage may be translated two ways:

Therefore my heart is sad, [that] when I found a man fully suited to me, [he was] unhappy, sad at heart, concealing [his] thought, planning **torment** under a blithe demeanor. Very often we two vowed that nothing except death alone would part us; **afterward** that is changed, now it is just as if our friendship never was. . . . The man commanded me to dwell in the grove of woods in the **cave** under the oak tree.

    or

Therefore my heart is sad, [that] when I found a man fully suited to me, [he was] unhappy, sad at heart, concealing [his] thought, planning **murder** under a blithe demeanor. Very often we two vowed that nothing except death alone would part us; that is changed **back**, now it is just as if our friendship never was. . . . The man commanded me to dwell in the grove of woods in the **grave** under the oak tree.

In the first translation, the speaker has been exiled to a cave in the woods by the man she loves, but she is very much alive. In the other, she has been murdered and is doomed to lie in the grave beneath the oak. Building on archaeological evidence showing that a significant number of execution sites are focused around barrows, Sarah Semple speculates that the speaker might be dead, executed for some crime. Since executed criminals are particularly likely to return from the dead, she concludes that the woman might be enduring "some kind of supernatural exile, a pagan afterlife, or, in a Christian view, a wretched living death."[63] Bruce Mitchell and Fred Robinson rather ruefully observe that "the narrative is sufficiently cryptic and the language of Old English sufficiently flexible that a case can be made for a variety of different situations in the poem," so that we will probably never know precisely what the poet originally meant.[64] Intriguingly, the differing translations are produced by the ambiguity of just three words in the text: *morþor, eft,* and *eorðscræf.*[65]

The first of these words, *morþor,* gives rise to the modern word "murder" and is often translated as such. However, in Old English it can also signify "crime, violence, torment." If the husband in the poem does *not* kill the speaker, he nevertheless sentences her to a life in lonely exile—in itself a kind of violence, and certainly a torment for her. Similarly, *eft* can signify both "afterward," looking forward in time as a consequence of an action, and "back," returning to a state before the action took place. *Morþor,* then, whether murder or exile, signals a drastic change of the woman's status: she is either exiled, abandoned, or dead.

But the most difficult word to reconcile is *eorðscræf,* which can either mean "cave" or "grave." Most translators prefer the former version, and *The Wife's Lament* is presented as a poem of exile. Yet *eorðscræf* is also used to signify the dragon's barrow in *Beowulf* (l. 3046)—a barrow that is clearly a grave. Archeological as well as etymological evidence supports the belief that the Anglo-Saxons did make an association between the *eorðscræf* and ancient barrows as places haunted by supernatural entities, but how deeply this belief pervaded the culture, we will never know.

In all these examples—dragons, demons, or *draugr*—there is a clear tendency to associate evil with the unquiet dead, with barrows and barrow-dwellers. The same pattern appears in *The Lord of the Rings*. As with the dragon in *Beowulf*, there is some difficulty over whether the barrow-wight is the revenant of the person for whom the barrow was originally built, or if it might have invaded the barrow somewhat later. If one accepts that the barrow-wight is indeed a *draugr,* then it would have to be the original occupant; *haugbúi* may have their faults, but I know of no instance where one took over another's barrow. This possibility leads to the horrifying prospect that "good can be turned to evil even after death, as in some branches of Classical mythology, which suggest that the dead all hate the living, even their own dearest relations, simply out of jealousy for life."[66]

But evidence from the text suggests that the barrow-wight is probably *not* the ghost of the original inhabitant. Tom Bombadil tells the hobbits that he was there before the kings and the graves and the barrow-wights, which implies that events occurred in that order—first the Kings, then the graves, and finally the barrow-wights. While one must certainly have barrows before one can have barrow-wights, most hauntings begin relatively soon after interment, not after the considerable passage of time implied by Bombadil's phrasing. Furthermore, he seems to remember the woman who was buried there, and he speaks well of her. The treasure clearly belonged to the people of Westernesse, eventually destroyed by the evil man who became none other than the Witch-King of Angmar (*FR*, I, viii, 142). Appendix A adds that the barrows were built in the First Age, before Men had crossed into Beleriand, which would make them very old indeed, and that implies that the wight is nothing more than "an opportunist who has moved . . . into someone else's abode" sometime later (*LR*, 1017). Furthermore, Merry's statement upon waking seems to indicate that he has somehow experienced the memories of one of these men. "'Of course, I remember!' he said. 'The men of Carn Dûm came on us at night, and we were worsted" (*FR*, I, viii, 140). Interpretations of this scene are many and varied; some have argued that these words prove Merry was possessed by the spirit of the King buried there; Flieger concludes that "the prince of

Cardolan actually if only momentarily inhabits Merry," who might be regarded as synonymous with Tom Shippey's "body in the barrow."[67] These
are certainly plausible interpretations. However, another possibility is that
Tolkien, perhaps unconsciously, was playing with the Guthlac stories and
allowing *his* barrow-dwellers, like Guthlac's demons, to falsely reclaim lost
glory and "slay" its enemies a second time. The great power of the Enemy,
after all, is to delude men and women into believing that which is not real.
Merry's statement confirms that the Men of Westernesse were the "innocent victims of treachery," but it does *not* necessarily mean that the wight
is the revenant of the person buried there.[68] Close inspection of Merry's
statement reveals that he says nothing warriors on either side of the battle
would not know. More important, though, is that allowing good souls to
be tormented in the afterlife is inconsistent with Tolkien's cosmology and
conflicts with images of death and the afterlife presented elsewhere.

There are, in fact, three sets of barrows in *The Lord of the Rings*: the
field of barrows on the Downs, the mounds of the Kings of Rohan, and,
more subtly, the Haunted Mountain, which the people of Rohan call the
Dwimorberg. *Dwimor* is simply Old English for "phantom, ghost," though
it can also mean "illusion" or "error." *Burg* means "dwelling within a forti-
fied enclosure" or "fort"—thus, Dwimorburg means, appropriately enough,
"ghost fort." But Tolkien's explicit translation of Dwimorburg as "Haunted
Mountain" also links *-burg* with *beorg*, "mountain, hill," or "mound, burial
place"—the root of our word "barrow"—which seems to allow for its interpretation as such. But only two of the three barrow-grounds are haunted.
The mounds of Rohan are peaceful; the people of Rohan place them on
the road leading to Edoras, so all visitors must pass by them, and there is
no indication that anyone is bothered by ghosts. Like the tomb of Balin,
or the Rath Dínen in Minas Tirith, their graves are peaceful and no threat
to the living. The mounds are hallowed places, made holy by the virtue of
the men interred in them; the Barrow-downs and the Haunted Mountain
are unhallowed, places the living have no business entering except by dire
necessity, and even then at great risk, as Baldor of Rohan discovered.

This distinction also suggests that those who are condemned to remain
on earth as spirits are guilty of some sin, haunting their enclosures until
their crimes can be atoned for or abnegated. For the Oathbreakers, the
transgression is obvious: they broke their word to Isildur—the greatest of

failings in the Icelandic sagas and in *Beowulf*—and therefore cannot rest until they have atoned for their wrongdoing by demonstrating loyalty to Isildur's heir. The barrow-wight's sin is less obvious, but something of its nature is suggested by its strong association with the Ringwraiths. In fact, early drafts of this chapter show Tolkien asking himself: "Are Black-riders actually horsed Barrow-wights?"[69] That idea was obviously discarded, but the barrow-wight never completely shook its association with the Nazgûl: *Unfinished Tales* reports that the wights were stirred up at the coming of the chief of the Ringwraiths, just as their armies were mustered at his command ages ago.[70] For although the identities of the individual Ringwraiths are largely unknown, we know that *this* Ringwraith is Angmar, the very King who betrayed the Men of Westernesse so long ago, and that "evil spirits out of Angmar and Rhudaur entered into the deserted mounds and dwelt there" after the Dunedain departed (*LR*, 1017). Just as the barrow-wight was a lesser man than Angmar in life, it has become a lesser wraith in death, still under the dominion of its perverted master, betrayed by its own treachery into an endless shadow-life. Although it is conjectural, it seems to me likely that the barrow-wight was originally some soldier from Carn Dûm fallen on the battlefield, reanimated and reembodied by the presence of his evil master and subject to his will.

In the medieval tradition, barrows are places ordinary people do not go, and Tolkien seems to add that ordinary people do not end up there, either. Frodo, Sam, Merry, and Pippin all escape the confines of the barrow, and they do so primarily because of the redemptive power of love and friendship. If Aragorn's forgiveness allows for the release of the Oathbreakers, Frodo's loyalty to his friends allows for their escape from the barrow. Where treachery led to an afterlife of suffering and damnation, faithfulness led to enduring friendship, thus demonstrating the ancient belief that love is stronger than death. Even the haunted places of Middle-earth suggest human souls are not forever confined in their tombs or monuments but make their way out of this world into the next, where they find at last a joy that is "more than memory" (*LR*, 1038). Hope may exist without guarantees, but it does exist.

In Tolkien's cosmology, there is a very specific origin for the unquiet dead. Those who linger, whose lives have been protracted until they have no meaning even to themselves, are invariably guilty of some crime or sin for which they must atone before they can find peace. The restless dead in Tolkien's fiction, the Oathbreakers and the barrow-wights, are those whose unpleasant deeds in life resulted in an unpleasant fate in death, and like Guthlac's demons or Beowulf's dragon they are forever bound by walls of earth. Other burials in *The Lord of the Rings* show that those who have committed no evil beyond the usual complement of faults and failings do not linger in their graves. For the vast majority of the peoples of Middle-earth, the mystery of what awaits beyond death remains hopeful. As Frodo discovers, simple, ordinary virtues like love, loyalty, and courage are enough to escape the barrow and the shadowy half-life within it. Wherever else the spirits of the departed go, they are not confined by walls of earth. And that, as Gandalf says elsewhere in *The Lord of the Rings,* may be an encouraging thought.

CHAPTER 5

Applicability

"Hope without Guarantees"

Much of American popular culture encourages us to overlook the existence of death. Contemporary cemeteries are often as flat as possible, calling no attention to the headstones and prompting us to look beyond the graves and toward the horizon. Hollywood perpetuates images of unchanging youth and perpetual beauty, portraying aging as disgraceful and dying as shameful. Even stories that purport to be about the dead, such as Charlaine Harris's vampire series or AMC's *The Walking Dead,* tend to gloss over the moment of death to focus on a sensationalized form of the afterlife. Again and again, the story society tells itself is one that relegates death to the background, that negates the power of death and makes dying a failure. The result is a society bereft of any means to understand the nature of death; there are no consistent messages about what death means or how to face it. The modern world has developed a culture "that desperately needs stories—perhaps even myths—about dying to provide some guides to appropriate roles and worthy behavior."[1]

Tolkien's mythology, quite simply, helps fulfill that need. While many authors flinch and turn away, Tolkien's story looks death directly in the face. When a character dies, someone else is there, watching those final moments with love and pity but without pretending that there will be a miraculous last-minute recovery or false certainty of what lies beyond death. *The Lord of the Rings* provides a blueprint for dying and for the roles the witnesses might assume as death approaches, and in so doing, it becomes what Kenneth Burke calls a "proverb writ large." Literature, says Burke, should present its readers with "typical, recurrent situations" encountered in real life and should therefore "apply beyond literature to life in general."[2] By showing death as both positive and negative, "the sweet and the bitter," Tolkien's text offers each of us the means to prepare for our own eventual ends (*RK*, VI, vi, 952).

Tolkien, of course, was deeply interested in how readers adapted and applied his story to their own lives, and he was not at all offended if that application took unusual forms. (His letters, for instance, reveal an almost childlike delight when a particular breeder wanted to give a line of her bulls Elvish names, even going so far as to invent names for her.[3]) For the most part, however, he took his work seriously, and he was more than a little offended at attempts to *mis*apply its messages or to apply it as an allegory (*LOTR*, xvii).

Tolkien's imaginary world exists mostly for enjoyment, of course, and is intended primarily to delight its readers. But it also provides a means of experiencing death not otherwise readily available. By pausing to linger with the dying, Tolkien's readers are able to rehearse the moment of death again and again, trying on various roles, finding out what feels right or "good" and then applying that lesson to their own lives. We have forgotten how to die, but *The Lord of the Rings* helps us remember.

Most scholars believe that fantastic literature frequently "operates as a mnemonic device that makes the forgotten or repressed reappear in the guise of an imagery by which the 'real' is connected with the unknown."[4] Death is both real *and* the ultimate unknown. The pages of *The Lord of the Rings* present that reality on a multitude of levels and make it if not familiar at least less utterly alien. The story encapsulates and adapts medieval conceptions of "good" and "bad" deaths: the basic tenet that death should ideally occur in the presence of friends and family, the notion that facing death with unflinching courage constitutes the highest form of heroism, the ideal that beyond death we shall find joy that is poignant as grief. For most of the twentieth century, these beliefs have existed in "an alternative or even oppositional relation to the dominant culture," though they are now beginning to reassert themselves in popular understanding.[5]

Of course, it might be, and has been, argued that *The Lord of the Rings* is only a fantasy, with no relation to real life, completely irrelevant to contemporary experience. But the very popularity of the book says otherwise. Because of a publication irregularity early in its history, no one knows exactly how many copies of *The Lord of the Rings* have been sold; some sources put the current number as high as 150 million.[6] Soldiers in Afghanistan carry its two-and-a-half-pound bulk with them as they deploy; ministers in the field use its passages to offer comfort to their struggling congregations; doctors and patients fighting desperate battles against lethal illnesses find symbolic healing in its pages. Significant numbers of medieval scholars owe their interest in the field to Tolkien's work.[7] All this suggests that *The Lord of the Rings* is far more than "just a fantasy"; it creates in modern audiences in "a feeling that his work addresses serious issues that demand a response not forthcoming from the official spokesmen of his and our culture."[8]

What Tolkien's work addresses directly is our knowledge, despite the prevailing myths, that we will die. It is all very well to assert that death and dying are nothing so serious when the promise of a happy afterlife is certain; it is far more difficult—and far more worthwhile—to offer comfort and consolation for the inevitability of death when no guarantees are offered. That is precisely what Tolkien's masterwork does. Whatever he believed in his waking life, in his fiction Tolkien provided his characters "no assurance of any future beyond death," no promise of a world to come or a joyful afterlife.[9] They have what we have, and hardly even that: "Death as part of the nature, physical and spiritual, of Man, and . . . Hope without guarantees."[10] But hope without guarantees is not no hope at all, and the promise of *The Lord of the Rings* is that each death, all deaths, mean something. Because it asserts that all deaths are significant and meaningful and that anyone can die like a hero, *The Lord of the Rings* functions as a proverb of consolation for the inevitability of death.

But the way is often hard, and nowhere does Tolkien insist that accepting death is easy. Dying will be our last significant act on this earth, and the way an individual faces the end of his or her life, in fiction or in reality, is the ultimate expression of character. Of course, not everyone has the luxury of knowing he or she is about to die, and not everyone who does regards such knowledge as a blessing. Most of us prefer not to think about it, but we know death can come at any time. Accidents happen; crimes occur; aneurysms and strokes whisk away life in a heartbeat. But for those who are granted the time to experience the process of dying, the knowledge that death is coming can be an enormous gift. Death is only meaningful if life is sacred, and its imminent presence makes the power and beauty of life stand out the clearer. Even in the depths of a war zone, honor and compassion are ranked among the highest of virtues; dignity and courage can be found in the cancer ward. As *The Lord of the Rings* attests, anyone can die like a hero.

For centuries, heroic death was an ideal limited to the elite of society, the kings and warriors whose lives constituted the raw material from which stories arose. Such a death presupposed a death in battle, fighting an intractable enemy against overwhelming odds. Facing the prospect of death gave the hero the opportunity to demonstrate his or her courage, loyalty, and determination, along with the willingness to sacrifice him- or herself for the greater good. Though undeniably built on the older, Greek models of the heroic code, our modern attitude toward heroes is more closely related to medieval conceptions. Achilleus dies, after all, primarily for himself: he fights before the walls of Troy not out of any sense of justice or honor but because he wants his name to live forever.[11] By the time Beowulf was written, things had changed; a good leader "dies for his people rather than a body of retainers dying for their leader; the concept of vengeance is replaced by that of sacrifice."[12] Beowulf certainly desires the immortality of fame, but he wants to be remembered for the deeds he accomplished *on behalf of his people*. Beorthnoth takes it one step further and dies not for fame or glory but for king and country. Slowly, the perception of what makes a hero has changed, though the underlying definitions of a heroic death have not. Nowadays, heroism is defined by those who die so that others might live, and whether or not "anyone else ever [knows] about it is beside the purpose" (*TT,* IV, viii, 692). In some respects, heroism is much humbler than once it was.

Nevertheless, it is still heroism. For all that Americans tend to regard the examples of Beowulf and Beorthnoth as quaint and outdated, the old values of achieving a heroic death are still very much in play. Though society may have changed in the past one thousand years, people have not. We still speak of "sacrificing oneself for one's country" or "dying like a hero." The president greets the return of troops from the field by praising "our heroes." Uniform white stones in the orderly rows of military cemeteries commemorate the loss of "fallen heroes." Ordinary men and women living in the eighth century, or the thirteenth, or the twenty-first, all admire the

bravery with which certain men and women have confronted death, sometimes succumbing, sometimes surviving, but always facing their own ends
with courage, dignity, and hope. It is no less true of Beowulf confronting
his dragon (the Anglo-Saxon symbol of death and decay) than it is for
soldiers today. In fact, heroes are often defined by the way they face their
deaths: "Heroism is first and foremost a reflex of the terror of death. We
admire the courage to face death; we give such valor our highest and most
constant adoration; it moves us deeply in our hearts because we have doubts
about how brave we would be. When we see a man bravely facing his own
extinction, we rehearse the greatest victory we can imagine."[13] It takes no
great stretch of the imagination, then, to understand why *The Lord of the
Rings* should appeal so strongly to contemporary warriors: it asserts that
they are heroes because they face death every day, and they do so bravely,
even when they come from a culture that regards warfare with suspicion. It
allows the men and women of the armed forces to place themselves within
an ancient tradition of heroic action, in which honor, courage, and sacrifice
are the highest of values. It resurrects the old values of the heroic code and
applies them to the lives of ordinary soldiers. It hallows both the glory and
horror of death in battle, the intrinsic honor bestowed on those who sacrifice their lives on behalf of others. And it allows readers to see something
of the hero in themselves.

The heroes of the old stories are, for the most part, larger than life; they
face challenges and monsters well beyond the scope of ordinary men and
women. But most of the heroes of *The Lord of the Rings* are recognizably
human: they falter, they doubt, they make mistakes. Théoden, who dies
in the purest example of the heroic death, does so only after a significant
failure: he almost allowed Saruman and the Uruk-hai to overrun his kingdom and destroy the people he was sworn to protect. Boromir redeems
himself after his failed attempt to wrest the Ring from Frodo. Aragorn
wrestles with doubt and uncertainty. Even Gandalf, the immortal Maia,
occasionally hesitates and makes mistakes. And the two principal heroes,
Frodo and Sam, are literally too small for the task put before them. Theirs
is a humbler kind of heroism, where "small hands do [great deeds] because
they must, while the eyes of the great are elsewhere" (*FR*, II, ii, 262). Yet
these two, the unlikeliest of heroes, succeed where no one else could. They
face death and destruction on a colossal scale, and they very nearly succumb

to the temptation to give in, to surrender, to just lie down and die. But they don't. They continue to push forward, right up to the bitter end. For contemporary soldiers, who face the very real prospect of death every day, the assurance that "the greatest warriors are often not the strongest of body, but the stoutest of heart; that the smallest and most docile ones are the very ones upon whose fate Middle Earth [sic] (and maybe our world?) can and does depend" must be comforting indeed.[14]

But *The Lord of the Rings* also acknowledges that in any war there are large numbers of casualties, enormous loss and suffering, huge amounts of destruction and annihilation. Tolkien, however, insists that while deaths in war may be inevitable, they are never insignificant or unimportant. Though thousands of unnamed soldiers die on the battlefields of Middle-earth, there is the persistent sense that each of them died honorably, fighting for a cause worth fighting for, and that therefore their deaths, their lives, were valuable and good. To die in battle was, after all, "the highest morality of the heroic honour-value," and if the memory of that honor was lost during the horrors of twentieth-century wars, perhaps it can be revived to prevent horrors in the twenty-first.[15]

Most of us, obviously, will not die on the field of battle, but that does not render us ineligible for heroic deaths. It must be remembered that even in the "heroic age" of Germanic history, heroic ideals were *ideals,* not reflections of reality. Given the vivid portrayals of heroic deaths in the old stories, it is easy to forget that "in reality the vast majority of deaths must have been from accident, disease or simply old age, the mourners bereft of redress or the comfort of glorious last words or deeds."[16] Most people, then as now, died from causes other than war. As the teachings of Christianity took hold, death in war came to be seen as less desirable, though the value of such a death did not completely disappear. Slowly, as the centuries passed, the old ideals expressed in literature merged with the more achievable ideals of the *ars moriendi,* slowly changing the definition of the heroic death.

In our own age, the traditions of the heroic death on the battlefield and the principle of the *ars moriendi* have merged into a new definition of heroic death. The old definition is, as we have seen, still very much with us, but the gradual adaptation of the centuries has located heroism in the sickbed as well as on the battlefield. The warrior ethic is echoed in phrases such as "fighting a valiant fight against cancer," "battling illness," or "facing suffering with courage." Such knowledge "offers the individual the chance to understand his/her life as standing outside the mundane concerns of everyday life, giving the individual the opportunity to define his/her own fate by engaging in moral behaviour, sacrifice, bravery and spiritual adventure in the service of a higher purpose."[17] The *ars moriendi* donates its presupposition that the dying person knows he or she is dying, allowing him or her the chance to say their last goodbyes and to make peace with the world they leave behind. We are witnessing, in our own time, "the development of a new art of dying," in which new approaches in medical care of the terminally ill meet the old values of compassion, family presence, and acceptance.[18]

Aragorn typifies this approach to death; though once he was a proud and noble warrior and has become a king, he dies simply because it is time to die. He has grown old, and there is no need for him to die in a blaze of glory. He does not die what we might call the "heroic death," but he *does* die a "good death," and the good death he exemplifies bears a distinct resemblance to a good death both as the *ars moriendi* and as modern people tend to define it. Therefore, he calls his family to him, expresses his final wishes, and then quietly, peacefully, passes away. Aragorn's story is repeated hundreds of times, in hospices, hospitals, and homes across America.

In fact, *The Lord of the Rings* is often cited in medical literature as a tool for coping with imminent death. For physicians and clergy, it is often promoted as a resource for understanding aging, dealing with grief, or even developing skills for better self-awareness (and, by logical extension, better awareness of others).[19] Psychiatrists note that "by mobilising the imagination and fantasy, literary works engage the reader more fully," which allows the reader to gain a new level of understanding of their suffering. Sometimes, they note, the uplifting effect of a good story can be enduring, as was the case of a Tolkien "devotee" who continued to be inspired by *The Lord of the Rings* until his death.[20] Arthur W. Frank encourages his patients to read stories such as *The Lord of the Rings,* which he specifically mentions, because it reminds them that "death is not a series of preventable illnesses; rather, life is an unpreventable death, and that is all right."[21] Radiation oncologist Nagraj Huigol believes that identifying with characters in stories like *The Lord of the Rings* can help patients in fighting against cancer, too.[22] An article in the *Journal of Clinical Oncology* recounts the case of a young woman suffering from advanced breast cancer. Instead of regretting the terminality of her condition, she joked with her doctors that she had developed the "Gollum look." But when they asked, probably with a certain alarm, if she was identifying with Gollum, she replied, "No, I'm Frodo after destroying the ring in Mount Doom, and the eagles have just swept down to carry Sam and I to safety. We're not sure yet where we are going, but it's got to be better than where we have been." Therefore, her doctors concluded, "*The Lord of the Rings* had clearly provided a lens through which our patient was enabled to interpret and deal with her cancer treatment experience."[23] The authors go on to propose a new method of patient treatment patterned after *The Lord of the Rings*.

In all these cases, the patient is encouraged to see him- or herself as the hero of the story and his or her own death as heroic. It does not necessarily guarantee the process will be easy or painless; patients and doctors alike know that being heroic sometimes means "making some hard decisions, dumping sentiment, [and] taking risks" that wouldn't be necessary in other situations.[24] Using *The Lord of the Rings* as a source of consolation and inspiration, patients and family members adapt the experiences of the characters of Tolkien's masterwork to fit their situations, just as the soldiers adapt the adventures of Frodo and Sam to suit theirs. Frodo dies in the end, of course, but not during the course of the story, and his suffering and sacrifice have earned him a sort of reprieve, a temporary release from the concerns of the world so that he can rest and recover before he travels beyond the circles of the earth. Even for the most terminal illness, there is the promise of rest on the other shore; even after the greatest of battles, peace can come again.

Even for those who have experienced less than ideal deaths, *The Lord of the Rings* offers consolation. It does not deny that some deaths occur due to tragedy, suicide, chance (if chance you call it), murder, or execution. But even for these, Tolkien holds out hope. In his cosmology, death is not the end but the beginning. Because Tolkien believed sentient spirits are by their very nature indestructible, no one ever faces the utter dissolution of their individuality.[25] Even Sauron might be saved in the end.

Tolkien continued to wrestle with the ultimate fate of his creations throughout his life, without reaching any clear conclusions. Later commentaries reveal that he was reluctant to condemn even the worst of his characters. By implication, the fates of ordinary persons who had died "bad" deaths could still be redeemed. Though such a philosophy might at first seem to fly in the face of the centuries of tradition, and in particular the tradition of the medieval Church, in reality it does not. Though suicides in particular had suffered "the most extreme form of bad death" and criminals were supposed to be denied interment in consecrated ground and endure perpetual excommunication, archaeological evidence shows that even these were occasionally buried within hallowed ground.[26] Even so, persons suffering from mental illness, extreme grief, or other infirmity could be judged as being *non compos mentis,* and thus still eligible for churchyard burial.[27] Compassion turns out to be more powerful than conformity. Suicides, like Denethor, and criminals, like Gollum and Gríma, will ultimately find their ways back to the One. The fate of those who suffer such ends is not, after all, the end of the story.

And in stories, the dead live again. In early medieval society, stories appear to have been the preferred mode of commemoration because "monuments may fall, but memory stands."[28] For the Anglo-Saxons, surrounded by the crumbling remains of Roman Britain, such a position must have seemed eminently logical. And, it must be conceded, in some ways their literature has proved to be more enduring than their architecture. Because their great halls and ordinary homes were built primarily of wood, little remains of their buildings in the archaeological record except post-holes and fire-pits.[29] No one builds houses "in the Anglo-Saxon style." Beowulf, if he ever actually existed at all, is remembered not because his barrow survives, but because the poem commemorating him does, at once "a memory and a memorial of the life of its hero, and a reminder to us that such memories are good and useful things."[30] To be commemorated in song was the highest form of veneration available to the early medieval hero, and if "memory was the sign of a good name" in the Middle Ages, it is no less so today.[31] We still speak of being "immortalized in song" or "famed in song and story." We "sing the praises" of people we admire or lament the sacrifice of the "unsung heroes" who fell, nameless, in battle.

In a keynote address to the Theatre of Memory Symposium, Irish president Michael D. Higgins points out that mythologies function as "a mechanism for the retention of hope in the unrealized possibilities of being human, truly free . . . with and for others."[32] It is in stories, and *only* in stories, that we can make the lives of the dead real and relevant to the present day. A monument not recognized as a monument is no monument at all; a building without a history is just a jumble of stones. Archaeological evidence attests to the existence of our ancestors; monuments call to mind the great exploits of the past and the names of those associated with them; memorials serve as a "material surrogate for the person departed."[33] But these are sterile endeavors until we connect the thing with the person, to "piece together this alternative side to the human story," as Mike Parker Pearson puts it.[34] Bones and buildings mean little unless they have a story attached.

Therefore, graves and monuments are important precisely because they connect the dead to their stories. The choices people make when choosing tombstones, whether for themselves or on behalf of those dear to them, says a great deal about the deceased's life, values, and personality. The graves of Middle-earth, coming directly from Tolkien's imagination, clearly reveal the cultures of the individuals interred within them. The sadness and beauty of the Elvish mounds speak not only to the loss of the individual within, but the passing of their entire culture; the durability of the Dwarves' stone monuments recalls the endurance and steadfastness of their people and the legends associated with them.

Perhaps the clearest testimony that his readers find comfort in Tolkien's writing appears in their final statements: their own gravestones. Most famous, of course, is Tolkien's own grave, which bears the names and emblems of Beren and Lúthien—a clear reference to the story that was at once private memory and public mythology. But ordinary readers also find comfort in Tolkien's words and wish to use them on their own headstones. One face of a gravestone in Ann Arbor, Michigan, reads simply "Never laugh at live dragons," complete with attribution to Bilbo Baggins—which makes one wonder about where the decedent met a dragon. In Llangynhafal, Wales, the phrase "All that is gold does not glitter" peeps through the grass of the headstone commemorating a woman who died in 1992. In the Rosehill Cemetery of Chicago, the reverse of a stone reads "A day will come at last when I / Shall take the hidden paths / that run west of the moon / east of the sun"—not quite Tolkien's line breaks, but certainly his wording. Yet another monument features an image of Gandalf, Frodo, and

Sam, with the phrase "My body lies, but still I roam," carved in Angerthas runes below. In each case, the words or images tell passersby something about the deceased; at the very least, one knows that he or she loved Tolkien's stories in life enough to carry them along into death. In other words, the viewer has begun to reconstruct the story of the departed. Tombstones thus serve as the ultimate plot synopsis.

Modern memorials, however, may also take less tangible forms, as populations become increasingly mobile and the Internet gains ever more widespread use. In the case of Tolkien devotees, forms of commemoration range from scholarship to storytelling, an appropriate legacy for a man who was both scholar and storyteller. The Tolkien Society, for instance, publishes the Peter Roe Memorial Booklets, an irregular series of journals that commemorate a talented member of the Society who was killed at the age of sixteen.[35] Topics of these journals range from travel in Middle-earth to the Sindarin Lexicon. For other writers, storytelling itself becomes both the memorial and the mode of commemoration. Increasingly, people set up websites for friends and family members to tell stories of their deceased loved ones. While the vast majority sites honor human beings, at least one commemorates the death of Blanco, the horse that played Shadowfax in Peter Jackson's movies.[36] Some sites use fiction as a means of both commemoration and healing. For instance, following the news of her friend's deteriorating condition due to ovarian cancer, an online fan fiction writer wrote a beautiful short story titled "Elanor of Westmarch: Grace," in which Sam's daughter Elanor nurses her mother Rose through her final days of life.[37] The story deals with grief and loss but, appropriately for Tolkien-based fan fiction, is not without an element of hope.

As in real life, the gravesites of Middle-earth are routinely connected with stories, either of the individual interred within or of the larger history in which he or she participated. But whereas graves in modern life are often regarded as the end of the story, graves in *The Lord of the Rings* are often the point where the story begins. The sight of the mounds of the Kings of Rohan prompts Aragorn to tell the tale of Rohan's beginnings and reminds us that the story, in fact, goes on. On Cerin Amroth, Frodo hears for the first time what his quest actually means, and he is granted a vision of what will come if he succeeds. Standing beside Balin's tomb, Frodo remembers Bilbo's tales of adventure with the fallen Dwarf. Boromir's story does not end with his funeral; later, his boat is seen by his brother Faramir as it journeys toward the sea.

But the tales of the restless dead are perhaps even more compelling, preying on our unconscious fears and desires about the afterlife. On the one hand, such stories are popular because they provide "proof," however tenuous, of life after death. On the other, they reflect an ancient fear that perhaps the afterlife will not be as pleasant or joyful as we imagine. Such appears to be the case of the ghosts of Middle-earth, bound to the loci of their tombs as a consequence for their own actions. But Tolkien's ghosts suggest that there is more to the story than that. From Frodo's encounter with the barrow-wight, on through Aragorn's summoning of the Oath-breakers, and into the tortuous paths of the Dead Marshes, there is a sub-tle but continual progression toward resolution. Frodo's encounter with the barrow-wight leads to the breaking of the grave; Aragorn's pact with the Oathbreakers severs their bonds to earth; the Dead in the Marshes have slipped beyond the reach of the Enemy. The ghosts of Middle-earth may have their origins in Sauron's manipulations, but none of them are bound to him forever; all of them are freed by perseverance, compassion, and courage. Once the unquiet dead have escaped from the burden of their shadowy half-lives, there is the undeniable sense of restoration and peace. They have gone to their rests, and the fact that even such terrible spirits as these yearn for the release of death suggests that most of us, who have done nothing nearly so terrible, should not fear death either.

Each time a character dies, we are reminded of our own inevitable deaths and invited to experience death with them. The deaths may be grand and heroic, penitential and moving, even sudden or unsettling—but so is death as it occurs in real life. Taken as a proverb, "the apparent contradictions" in *The Lord of the Rings* "depend upon differences in *attitude,* involving a correspondingly different choice of *strategy.*"[38] Like all free creatures, we are given a choice: we can face death with courage and dignity, or we can kill ourselves in pride and defiance, but the choice is ours. Anyone can choose between Théoden and Denethor, Gandalf and Gríma, Boromir and Gol-lum. And therein lies our hope.

No one knows what awaits us beyond death, or if there is anything that follows at all. Such a matter is and always has been the province of faith. As a Christian, Tolkien certainly *believed* in the promise of a joyful afterlife, and his characters repeatedly express that belief. Théoden speaks of reunion with his ancestors; the Elves look to the Younger Children for their final salvation; Aragorn looks forward to the joy beyond the circles of the world, where we shall have more than memory. But none of them *know*. Tolkien did not *know*. That is precisely the point. All that we *know* is that we will die, and that knowledge, paradoxically, is what gives life its urgency, what inspires us to create and to love and to *be*. "To live at all, you have to bet your life," writes Frank McConnell, and Tolkien would doubtless have agreed.[39] Despite the risks, it is the only thing to do.

Of course, there is every possibility that we, like Frodo, will fail. It matters less that we succeed than that we make the attempt and trust in Providence to do the rest. Tolkien realized quite clearly that the world does not need many of the grand heroes of epic and legend, but it has an enormous need for the humbler heroes of folktales and fairy-story. In the pages of *The Lord of the Rings,* we are encouraged to live life joyfully and to accept death hopefully. Throughout the book, the characters, the land-scape, and even the dead of Middle-earth teach us that death is not the end but the beginning, "the origin and the goal of any meaning we may choose to call human."[40] To live a life of faith, to believe in things unseen, to value freedom, honor, love, and friendship beyond all things—these are the ideals that give life meaning and poignancy. Whatever else it may be, death is not the end of the story. For the characters of *The Lord of the Rings* as well as for us, the final destination is a mystery. What they do have, what we have, is hope.

Permissions Acknowledgments

Notes

INTRODUCTION

1. Dustin C. Holcomb, "A Soldier's Tribute," *Stryker Brigade News,* Dec. 28, 2004, accessed Jan. 11, 2006, http://www.strykernews.com/archives/2004/12/28/a_soldiers_tribute.html, site discontinued.

2. Robert A. Wise, "The Things They Wrote," *New York Times,* Mar. 21, 2004.

3. *The Lord of the Rings* was and remains fairly difficult to classify; various critics have called it a novel, a romance, a fantasy, an epic, and a fairy tale. I have chosen Tolkien's own term, "fairy-story," which he defines as a story that deals with marvelous events but must be treated as if these marvels are completely believable within the world in which the occur. See J. R. R. Tolkien, "On Fairy-Stories," in *The Monsters and the Critics and Other Essays,* ed. Christopher Tolkien (New York: HarperCollins, 1988), 117.

4. R. J. Gore, "Some Spiritual Lessons from *The Lord of the Rings:* Prayer Breakfast 84th Combat Engineers (Heavy)," Oct. 14, 2004, sermon, Strider172's Xanga Site: Back in the Shire. Was: From Mordor Where the Shadows Lie, accessed Jan. 12, 2006, http://xanga.com/strider172, site discontinued.

5. J. R. R. to Joanna de Bortadano, ca. Apr. 1956, draft, in *The Letters of J. R. R. Tolkien,* ed. Humphrey Carpenter (New York: Houghton Mifflin, 2000), 246.

6. J. R. R. Tolkien, forward to the second edition, *The Lord of the Rings* (New York: Houghton Mifflin, 1994), xvii.

7. See Kenneth Burke, *The Philosophy of Literary Form: Studies in Symbolic Action,* third edition, (Berkeley: Univ. of California Press, 1967), 296.

8. Suzanne Bell, *Encyclopedia of Forensic Science* (New York: Facts on File Books, 2004), 87.

9. Raymond Williams, *Marxism and Literature* (New York: Oxford Univ. Press, 1977), 122.

10. Quoted by Richard C. West in "The Interlace and Professor Tolkien: Medieval Narrative Technique in *The Lord of the Rings*," *Orcrist* 1 (1966): 32.

1. THE WAGES OF HEROISM

1. J. R. R. Tolkien to Joanna de Bortadano, ca. Apr. 1956, draft, and Tolkien to Rhona Beare, Oct. 14, 1958, both in *The Letters of J. R. R. Tolkien,* ed. Humphrey Carpenter, (New York: Houghton, Mifflin, 1981), 246, 284. W. A. Senior has argued the concept that subsumes the others is "the sustained and grieved sense of loss, of which death is but one form," but, if one were feeling particularly cantankerous, one could also argue that the loss of Gondolin, the Istari, the Elves, and beauty itself is but another form of death. W. A. Senior, "Loss Eternal in J. R. R. Tolkien's Middle-earth," in *J. R. R. Tolkien and His Literary Resonances: Views of Middle-earth,* eds. George Clark and Daniel Timmons, (Westport, CT: Greenwood, 2000), 173.

2. Plato, *Phaedo,* in *The Great Dialogues of Plato,* ed. Eric H. Warmington and Philip G. Rouse, trans. W. H. D. Rouse (New York: New American Library, 1956), 466; Matt 5:18, 24:35; Mark 13:31; Luke 16:17, 21:33; 2 Peter 3:10; Rev 21:1, RSV.

3. Mary Catharine O'Connor, *The Art of Dying Well: The Development of the* Ars Moriendi (New York: Columbia Univ. Press, 1942; authorized facsimile, Ann Arbor, MI: Univ. Microfilms, 1967), 5.

4. See David William Atkinson, *The English* Ars Moriendi (New York: Peter Lang, 1992), xi.

5. See Douglas J. Davies, *A Brief History of Death* (Malden, MA: Blackwell, 2005), 71–73.

6. Julie Beck, "What Good Is Thinking about Death?" *Atlantic,* May 28, 2015, http://www.theatlantic.com/health/archive/2015/05/what-good-is-thinking -about-death/394151. See Christopher A. Klinger et al., "Barriers and Facilitators to Care for the Terminally Ill: A Cross-Country Case Comparison Study of Canada, England, Germany, and the United States," *Palliative Care* 28 no. 2 (2013): 111–20, 116–17; see also Barbara Kreling et al., "'The Worst Thing about Hospice Is That They Talk about Death': Contrasting Hospice Decisions and Experience among Immigrant Central and South American Latinos with U.S.-Born, White, Non-Latino Cancer Caregivers," *Palliative Medicine* 24, no. 4 (2010): 427–34, for an interesting perspective on various cultures operating within U.S. borders.

7. Nancy Caciola, "Spirits Seeking Bodies: Possession and Communal Memory in the Middle Ages," in *The Place of the Dead: Death and Remembrance in Late Medieval and Early Modern Europe,* ed. Bruce Gordon and Peter Marshall (New York: Cambridge Univ. Press, 2003), 75.

8. See Nancy Beaty, *The Craft of Dying: A Study in the Literary Tradition of the* Ars Moriendi *in England* (New Haven: Yale Univ. Press, 1970) 2; and Atkinson, *English* Ars Moriendi, xi.

9. John M. Hill, *The Anglo-Saxon Warrior Ethic: Reconstructing Lordship in Early English Literature.* (Gainesville: Univ. Press of Florida, 2000), 1.

10. See Tom Shippey, *The Road Goes Ever On: How J. R. R. Tolkien Created a New Mythology,* (New York, Houghton Mifflin, 2003), 117, 124, 126, 130–31; see also his chapter "Goths and Romans in Tolkien's Imagination," in *J. R. R. Tolkien: The Forest and the City,* ed. Helen Conrad-O'Briain and Gerard Hynes (Portland, OR: Four Courts Press, 2013), 19–32, for an interesting perspective on the Gothic contributions to Tolkien's world.

11. Roy M. Luizza, "Beowulf: Monuments, Memory, History," in *Readings in Medieval Texts: Interpreting Old and Middle English Literature,* ed. David Johnson and Elaine Treharne, (Oxford: Oxford Univ. Press, 2005), 94.

12. Janet Brennan Croft, *War and the Works of J. R. R. Tolkien* (Westport, CT: Praeger: 2004), 146.

13. Theodore M. Andersson, *The Growth of the Medieval Icelandic Sagas (1180–1280)* (Ithaca, NY: Cornell Univ. Press, 2006), 37.

14. Karen Rockow, "Funeral Customs in Tolkien's Trilogy," *Unicorn* 3, no. 1 (1973): 27.

15. The events described in the *Chronicle* began in 755 or 757 but did not reach their climax until 786.

16. Jocelyn Wogan-Brown, "The Hero in Christian Reception," in *Old English Literature: Critical Essays,* ed. R. M. Liuzza (New Haven: Yale Univ. Press, 2002), 229.

17. Rolf H. Bremmer Jr., "Old English Heroic Literature," in Johnson and Treharne, *Readings in Medieval Texts,* 87.

18. *The* Beowulf *Manuscript: Complete Texts and* The Fight at Finnsburg, ed. and trans. R. D. Fulk (Cambridge, MA: Harvard Univ. Press, 2010), ll. 2513, 1387–89, 445–51. *Wyrce se þe mote / domes ær deaþe; þæt bið driht-guman / unlifgendum æfter selest.* [let him who can seek glory before death; that is the best afterward for a lifeless warrior].

19. Guy Bourquin, "The Lexis and Deixis of the Hero in Old English Poetry," in *Heroes and Heroines in Medieval English Literature: A Festschrift Presented to André Crépin on the Occasion of His Sixty-fifth Birthday,* ed. Leo Carruthers (Cambridge, UK: D. S. Brewer, 1994), 2, 3.

20. J. R. R. Tolkien, *Valaquenta,* in *The Silmarillion* (Boston: Houghton Mifflin, 1977), 31.

21. The Harry Potter series, of course, has altered this perception; it will be interesting to see if J. K. Rowling's books have effected a permanent change.

22. Richard Kieckhefer, *Magic in the Middle Ages* (1990; repr., Cambridge: Cambridge Univ. Press, 2003), 50.

23. *Gísli Sursson's Saga,* in *The Sagas of the Icelanders,* trans. Martin S. Regal (New York: Viking, 2000), 525.

24. John Milton, *Paradise Lost,* ed. Gordon Teskey (New York: Norton, 2005), I.63.

25. See Ilúvatar's words to the Ainur: "I have kindled you [i.e., created you, made you live] with the Flame Imperishable"; and "Ilúvatar shall give to their thoughts the secret fire" [i.e., make their thoughts live] (*Silm,* 15, 16). In *The Book of Lost Tales I,* the power of the Secret Fire is even more explicit. It is called "the Secret Fire that giveth Life and Reality" and "the fire that giveth Life and Reality" (53, 55). Note also Melkor's desire to possess the Flame Imperishable, in order to make beings of his own (16).

26. Matthew Dickerson, *Following Gandalf: Epic Battles and Moral Victory in The Lord of the Rings* (Grand Rapids, MI: Brazos, 2003), 229.

27. Tolkien to Robert Murray, SJ, Nov. 4, 1954, in *Letters,* 202; original emphasis.

28. Tolkien to Michael Straight, undated draft [probably written in Jan. or Feb. 1956], in *Letters,* 237.

29. Steven Mark Deyo, "Wyrd and Will: Fate, Fatalism, and Free Will in the Northern Elegy and J. R. R. Tolkien," *Mythlore* 53 (Spring 1988): 61.

30. Richard Purtill, *J. R.R. Tolkien: Myth, Morality, and Religion* (San Francisco, CA: Ignatius, 1984), 118.

31. Tolkien to Straight, draft, 237.

32. Dickerson, *Following Gandalf,* 215.

33. What he actually says is "For though I do not ask for aid, we need it" (*FR,* II, ii, 261).

34. *Grettir's Saga,* ed. and trans. Denton Fox and Herman Pálsson (Toronto: Univ. of Toronto Press, 1974), x.

35. Martin Puhvel, "The Concept of Heroism in the Anglo-Saxon Epic," in *La funzione dell'eroe germanico: storicita', metafora, paradigma: atti del Convegno internazionale di studio, Roma, 6-8 maggio 1993,* ed. Teresa Pàroli (Rome, Italy: Calamo, 1995), 71.

36. R. W. Hanning, "Prudential Penance," *Enarratio* 16 (2009): 20.

37. Edward Risden, "Plowing, Bowing, Burning, Journeying: Penance and Subverting Penance in Medieval Literature," *Enarratio* 16 (2009): 112.

38. See Phillipe Ariēs, *The Hour of Our Death: The Classic History of Western Attitudes toward Death over the Last One Thousand Years,* trans. Helen Weaver (1977; repr., New York: Barnes & Noble Press, 2000), 17.

39. Patricia Reynolds, "Funeral Customs in Tolkien's Fiction," *Mythlore* 27 (Spring 1993): 46.

40. J. R. R. Tolkien, "On Fairy-Stories," in *The Monsters and the Critics and Other Essays,* ed. Christopher Tolkien (New York: HarperCollins, 1988), 153.

41. Whether people actually did is a matter of some debate. Although Johan Huizinga asserted that "an everlasting call of memento mori resounds through life" in the Middle Ages (*The Waning of the Middle Ages: A Study of the Forms of Life, Thought, and Art in France and the Netherlands in the Dawn of the Renaissance* [1949; repr., New York: Anchor, 1989], 138), Douglas Gray points out that "the men of the Middle Ages did not spend all their waking moments thinking upon their end" (*Themes and Images in the Medieval English Religious Lyric* [London: Routledge & Kegan Paul 1972], 176). There seems no reason to assume that people living in the Middle Ages were substantially different from us: they thought about dying sometimes, and if they thought about it rather more often than we tend to now, it was likely because they were confronted with it that much more often.

42. William Caxton, *Here begynneth a lityll treatise shorte and abredged spekynge of the arte [and] crafte to knowe well to dye* (Westminster: 1490).

43. Tolkien, "On Fairy-Stories," 153.

2. THE BITTER END

1. See Nancy Caciola, "Spirits Seeking Bodies: Possession and Communal Memory in the Middle Ages," in *The Place of the Dead: Death and Remembrance in Late Medieval and Early Modern Europe,* ed. Bruce Gordon and Peter Marshall (2000; repr., New York: Cambridge Univ. Press, 2003), 75–76.

2. Phillippe Ariès. *The Hour of Our Death: The Classic History of Western Attitudes toward Death over the Last One Thousand Years,* trans. Helen Weaver (1977; repr., New York: Barnes & Noble Press, 2000), 12; L. M. Cohen, "Suicide, Hastening Death, and Psychiatry," *Archives of Internal Medicine* 158 (Oct. 1998): 1973.

3. Alexander Murray, *Suicide in the Middle Ages,* vol. 2 of 2, *The Curse of Self-Murder* (Oxford: Oxford Univ. Press, 2000), 317, 224.

4. Tom Shippey, *The Road Goes Ever On: How J. R. R. Tolkien Created a New Mythology* (New York: Houghton Mifflin, 2003), 165.

5. J. R. R. Tolkien, "The Homecoming of Beorthnoth," in *The Tolkien Reader* (New York: Ballantine, 1966), 21. Other scholars have taken a somewhat gentler approach; Shippey, for instance, points out that the word could mean

something more like "too much courage" (Tom Shippey, "Tolkien and 'The Homecoming of Beorhtnoth,'" in *Roots and Branches: Selected Essays on Tolkien by Tom Shippey,* ed. Peter Buchs, Thomas Honegger, and Andrew Moglestue. [Zurich: Walking Tree Publishers, 2007], 331), while Bernard Huppé opts for "vainglory" (Huppé, "The Concept of the Hero in the Early Middle Ages," in *Concepts of the Hero in the Middle Ages and the Renaissance,* ed. Norman T. Burns and Christopher Reagan [Albany: State Univ. of New York Press, 1975], 17) and Morton Bloomfield suggests it might be more like its German cognate *Übermut,* "high spirits" (Bloomfield, "Beowulf, Byrhtnoth, and the Judgment of God: Trial by Combat in Anglo-Saxon England," *Speculum* 64 [Oct. 1969]: 547).

6. Conventionally, scholars spell his name "Byrhtnoth," apparently due to the influence of *The Battle of Maldon.* The Petersborough version of the Anglo-Saxon Chronicle uses Byrihthoð and the Canterbury manuscript Byrtnoth (it also gives the wrong date). Tolkien corrects the spelling of the poem back to "Beorthnoth" (*beorth* = "bright"; *noth* = boldness, daring). See George Clark's chapter, "Tolkien and the True Hero," in *J. R. R. Tolkien and His Literary Resonances: Views of Middle-earth,* ed. George Clark and Daniel Timmons (Westport, CT: Greenwood, 2000), 49. Since this book is about Tolkien, I am using his spelling.

7. See Katherine O'Brien O'Keefe, "Heroic Values and Christian Ethics" in *The Cambridge Companion to Old English Literature,* edited by Malcolm Godden and Michael Lapidge (1991; repr., Cambridge: Cambridge Univ. Press, 2005), 107–25.

8. Bruce Mitchell, "'Until the Dragon Comes' . . . Some Thoughts on Beowulf," *Neophilologus* 47, no. 2 (1963): 131.

9. See Jean La Fontain, "Explaining Suicide: An Afterward," *Culture, Medicine, and Psychiatry* 36 (June 2012): 412.

10. Shippey, *Road Goes Ever On,* 158 (my emphasis).

11. Murray, *Curse of Self-Murder,* 317.

12. Ibid., 379, 321.

13. Richard Purtill, *J. R. R. Tolkien: Myth, Morality, and Religion* (San Francisco: Ignatius, 1984).

14. See Gandalf's reaction, *RK,* VI, vii, 836. Faramir's reaction is not recorded, but there is some reference to potential grief in "The Steward and the King" *RK,* VI, v, 938.

15. Yvette Kisor, "'Poor Sméagol': Gollum as Exile in *The Lord of the Rings,*" in *Tolkien in the New Century: Essays in Honor of Tom Shippey,* ed. John Wm. Houghton et al. (Jefferson, NC: McFarland, 2014), 157.

16. Nancy Caciola, "Wraiths, Revenants, and Ritual in Medieval Culture," *Past and Present* 152 (Aug. 1996): 15.

17. *Eyrbyggja Saga,* trans. Herman Pálsson and Paul Edwards (New York: Penguin, 1989), 93–95.

18. John D. Rateliff, *The History of the Hobbit,* pt. 1, *Mr. Baggins* (Boston: Houghton Mifflin, 2007), 187n8.

19. *Grettir's Saga,* trans. Denton Fox and Hermann Pálsson (Toronto: Univ. of Toronto Press, 1974), 79.

20. Marjorie Burns, "Night-Wolves, Half-Trolls, and the Dead Who Won't Stay Down," in Houghton et al., *Tolkien in the New Century Musics,* 192.

21. E. J. Christie, "Sméagol and Déagol: Secrecy, History, and Ethical Subjectivity in Tolkien's World," *Mythlore* 31 (Spring–Summer 2013): 95.

22. Walter Scheps, "The Fairy Tale Morality of *The Lord of the Rings,*" in *A Tolkien Compass,* ed. Jared Lobdell (La Salle, IL: Open Court, 1975), 51.

23. J. R. R. Tolkien to Michael Straight, Jan. or Feb. 1956, draft, *The Letters of J. R. R. Tolkien,* ed. Humphrey Carpenter (New York: Houghton Mifflin, 2000), 234.

24. Ibid.; Tolkien to Miss J. Burn, July 26, 1956, and Tolkien to Mrs. Eileen Elgar, Sept. 1963, draft, both in *Letters,* 252, 327.

25. Carol Fry, "Two Musics about the Throne of Ilúvatar: Gnostic and Manichaean Dualism in *The Silmarillion*" *Tolkien Studies* 12 (2015): 87.

26. Paul Kocher, *Master of Middle-earth: The Fiction of J. R. R. Tolkien* (New York: Ballantine, 1972), 31–32.

27. Tolkien to Elgar, draft, 327.

28. Tolkien to Amy Ronald, Dec. 15, 1956 , in *Letters,* 255.

29. Verlyn Flieger, *Interrupted Music: The Making of Tolkien's Mythology* (Kent, OH: Kent State Univ. Press, 2005), 142.

3. SONGS AND STONES

1. Mike Parker Pearson, *The Archaeology of Death and Burial* (College Station: Texas A&M Univ. Press, 1999), 193.

2. Ibid., 124.

3. J. D. C. Harte, "Law after Death, or 'Whose Body Is It?' The Legal Framework for the Disposal and Remembrance of the Dead," *Ritual and Remembrance: Responses to Death in Human Societies,* ed. John Davies (Sheffield, England: Sheffield Academic Press, 1994), 235.

4. Eva Reimers, "Death and Identity: Graves and Funerals as Cultural Communication," *Mortality* 4, no. 2 (1999): 147.

5. Victoria Thompson, *Dying and Death in Later Anglo-Saxon England* (Suffolk, England: Boydell, 2004), 159; Phillippe Ariès, *The Hour of Our Death: The*

Classic History of Western Attitudes toward Death over the Last One Thousand Years, trans. Helen Weaver (1977; repr., New York: Barnes & Noble Press, 2000), 340.

6. Karen Rockow, "Funeral Customs in Tolkien's Trilogy," *Unicorn* 3, no. 1 (1973): 22.

7. The cremation of Denethor is an exception; it *is* viewed negatively but, as discussed in chapter 2, primarily because it is a suicide and attempted murder, not because cremation is reprehensible in itself.

8. J. R. R. Tolkien, *Beowulf: A Translation and Commentary,* ed. Christopher Tolkien (New York: Houghton Mifflin Harcourt, 2014), 163.

9. See J. S. Ryan, "German Mythology Applied: The Extension of Literary Folk Memory," *Folklore* 77 no. 1 (Spring 1966): 45–59. See also C. L. Wrenn, *Beowulf* (London: Harrap, 1973).

10. Stephen Mitchell, "Memory, Mediality, and the 'Performative Turn': Recontextualizing Remembering in Medieval Scandinavia," *Scandinavian Studies* 85 (Fall 2013): 283.

11. Douglas Keister, *Stories in Stone: A Field Guide to Cemetery Symbolism and Iconography* (New York: MJF Books, 2004), 11.

12. Renate Lachmann, "Cultural Memory and the Role of Literature," *European Review* 12, no. 2 (2004): 172.

13. David L. Dettman, "Väinämöinen in Middle-earth: The Pervasive Presence of the Kalevala in the Bombadil Chapters of *The Lord of the Rings,*" in *Tolkien in the New Century: Essays in Honor of Tom Shippey,* ed. John Wm. Houghton et al. (Jefferson, NC: McFarland, 2014), 203.

14. Tolkien, *Beowulf,* 347.

15. Paul Kocher, however, reads it differently; see *Master of Middle-earth Kocher: The Fiction of J. R. R. Tolkien* (New York: Ballantine, 1972), 202–3.

16. See also J. R. R. Tolkien, *Return of the Shadow,* vol. 6 of *The History of Middle-earth,* ed. Christopher Tolkien (New York: Houghton Mifflin, 1988), 39, 241, 247–48; J. R. R. Tolkien to H. Cotton Michin, circa April 1956, draft, *The Letters of J. R. R. Tolkien,* ed. Humphrey Carpenter (New York: Houghton Mifflin, 2000), 294.

17. J. R. R. Tolkien, "Amroth and Nimrodel," in *History of Galadriel and Celeborn,* 240, in *Unfinished Tales* (Boston: Houghton Mifflin, 1980), 246; on the possibility that the idea was originally Nimrodel's, see 255n17.

18. Helen Conrad-O'Briain and Gerard Hynes, introduction to *J. R. R. Tolkien: The Forest and the City,* ed. Helen Conrad-O'Briain and Gerard Hynes (Portland, OR: Four Courts, 2013), 18.

19. At least, in Middle-earth, the trees are unique to Lothlórien; they seem to have been brought to Númenor from the West by the Elves (see *Unfinished Tales,* 167–68).

20. *Flet* is Old English for "floor," which is essentially all that it is: a platform without walls or railing, though there is a light screen that can be moved to block out the wind.

21. Douglas J. Davies, *A Brief History of Death* (Malden, MA: Blackwell, 2005), 128–29.

22. Susan Drury, "Funeral Plants and Flowers in England: Some Examples," *Folklore* 105 (1994): 101–3.

23. Andrew Reynolds, "The Definition and Ideology of Anglo-Saxon Execution Sites and Cemeteries," in *Death and Burial in Medieval Europe: Papers of the "Medieval Europe Brugge 1997" Conference*, vol. 2 of 11, ed. Guy De Boe and Frans Verhaeghe (Zellik, Belgium: I. A. P. Rapporten 2, 1997), 38.

24. See Lewis Spence, *British Fairy Origins* (London: Watts, 1946), 98–108.

25. Marjorie Burns, "Bridges, Gates, and Doors," in *Perilous Realms: Celtic and Norse Mythology in Tolkien's Middle-earth* (Toronto: Univ. of Toronto Press, 2005), 70.

26. Verlyn Flieger, *A Question of Time: J. R. R. Tolkien's Road to Faërie* (Kent, OH: Kent State Univ. Press, 1997), 22.

27. Tolkien to Humphrey Carpenter, 1955, in *Letters*, 221.

28. The proper spelling of this race is highly problematic, and Tolkien is inconsistent (See Tolkien to the editor of the *Observer* [James Louis Garvin], Feb. 20, 1938, in *Letters*, 31 and *The Peoples of Middle-earth*, vol. 12 of *The History of Middle-earth*, ed. Christopher Tolkien [New York: Houghton Mifflin, 1996], 24). For convenience, I shall use "dwarfs" when speaking of tradition and folklore and "Dwarves" when referring to those of Tolkien's creation.

29. Snorri Sturluson, *Edda*, trans. and ed. Anthony Faulkes (1986; repr., North Clarendon, VT: Turtle Publishing, 1995), 16.

30. J. R. R. Tolkien, in "The Nauglafring," in *The Book of Lost Tales II*, Vol. 2 of *The History of Middle-earth*, ed. Christopher Tolkien (New York: Houghton Mifflin, 1984), 247.

31. Michael D. C. Drout, "The Tower and the Ruin: The Past in J. R. R. Tolkien's Works," in Conrad O'Briain and Hynes, *The Forest and the City*, 186–87.

32. Tolkien, *Peoples of Middle-earth*, 301, 322, 383.

33. Ibid., 391n24.

34. For a fuller elucidation on Tolkien's development of the fate of the Dwarves after death, see John D. Rateliff's *The History of the Hobbit*, part 2, *The Return to Bag-End* (New York: Houghton Mifflin, 2007), 720.

35. See J. R. R. Tolkien, "The Later Annals of Beleriand," in *The Lost Road and Other Writings*, vol. 5 of *The Histories of Middle Earth* (New York: Houghton Mifflin, 1987). Again, for further discussion, see Rateliff's commentary in *The History of the Hobbit*.

36. Tolkien, *Peoples of Middle-earth*, 383, 384.

37. Durin's tomb is not described at all. Thorin is buried under the Lonely Mountain; all we know of his burial is that the Arkenstone lies upon his breast and that the Elven sword Orcrist lies atop the tomb (see *Hobbit,* 290; *FR,* II, iii, 272).

38. Nigel Saul, *English Church Monuments in the Middle Ages: History and Representation* (Oxford: Oxford Univ. Press, 2011), 154.

39. Although some people tend to regard the hobbits as a separate race, Tolkien states explicitly that the hobbits are a branch of the human race (Tolkien to Milton Waldman, ca. late 1951, in *Letters* 158).

40. Tom Shippey, *The Road Goes Ever On: How J. R. R. Tolkien Created a New Mythology* (New York: Houghton Mifflin, 2003), 117; see also Simone Bonechi, "'In the Mounds of Mundburg': Death, War and Memory in Middle-earth," in *The Broken Scythe: Death and Immortality in the Works of J. R. R. Tolkien,* ed. Roberto Arduini and Claudio A. Testi (Zurich: Walking Tree Publishers, 2012), 145.

41. See Christopher Tolkien's notes in "The Commentary on *The Cottage of Lost Play,*" in Tolkien, *Book of Lost Tales,* 22–25; and the *Quenta* in J. R. R. Tolkien's *The Shaping of Middle-earth,* vol. 4 of *The History of Middle-earth,* ed. Christopher Tolkien (New York: Houghton Mifflin, 1986), 199–200.

42. Strophe 92 reads:

Hwær cwom mearg? Hwær cwom mago? Hwær cwom maþþumgyfa?
Hwær cwom symbla gesetu? Hwær sindon seledreamas? (ll. 92–93)

["Where has gone the horse? Where has gone the warrior? Where has gone the giver of treasures?

Where has gone the banquet-place? Where have gone the joys of the hall?"] But the poem ends with *frofre to Fæder on heofonum, þær us eal seo fæstnung stondeð* [comfort from the Father in heaven, where for us all that is permanent stands]; my translation.

43. Christopher Daniell and Victoria Thompson, "Pagans and Christians: 400–1150," in *Death in England: An Illustrated History,* ed. Peter C. Jupp and Clare Gittings (New Brunswick, NJ: Rutgers Univ. Press, 2000), 68.

44. Anders Andrén, "Places, Monuments, and Objects: The Past in Ancient Scandinavia," *Scandinavian Studies* 85 (Fall 2013): 272.

45. Elizabeth Jane Stern, *Legends of the Dead in Medieval and Modern Iceland* (Ann Arbor, MI: Univ. Microforms International, 1987), 27, 12.

46. R. M. Luizza, "Beowulf: Monuments, Memory, History," in *Readings in Medieval Texts: Interpreting Old and Medieval English Literature,* ed. David Johnson and Elaine Treharne (Oxford: Oxford Univ. Press, 2005), 95.

47. See Howard Williams, *Death and Memory in Early Medieval Britain* (Cambridge: Cambridge Univ. Press, 2006), 124; and C. Lee, *Feasting the Dead: Food and Drink in Anglo-Saxon Rituals* (Woodbridge: Suffolk, Boydell, 2007).

48. Bonechi, "In the Mounds of Mundburg," 147.

49. Christopher Tolkien noticed this omission, and Wayne Hammond and Christina Scull restored it to the text by in the fiftieth anniversary edition (*TT,* III, viii, 545).

50. Rockow, "Funeral Customs in Tolkien's Trilogy," 29.

51. Patricia Reynolds, "Funeral Customs in Tolkien's Fiction," *Mythlore* 72 (Spring 1993): 50.

52. Hilda Roderick Ellis Davidson, "The Hill of the Dragon," *Folklore* 61 (Dec. 1950): 169.

53. Tolkien, *Beowulf,* 151.

54. See A. Tyler and H. Major, *The Early Anglo-Saxon Cemetery and Later Saxon Settlement at Springfield Lyons, Essex* (Chelmsford: Essex City Council, 2005); also Williams, *Death and Memory* 147–48; also his entry in the 2011 *Oxford Handbook of Anglo-Saxon Archaeology,* ed. Helena Hamerow, David A. Hinton, and Sally Crawford (Oxford: Oxford Univ. Press), "Mortuary Practices in Early Anglo-Saxon England," 238–65.

55. Joanna Scutts, "Battlefield Cemeteries, Pilgrimage, and Literature after the First World War: The Burial of the Dead," *English Literature in Transition* 52 no. 4 (2009): 393.

56. His precise knowledge of the custom is reflected in his commentary on *Beowulf,* 150–52.

57. Barbara I. Gusick, "The Ultimate Nothing: Death and the End of Work in Late-Medieval English Lyrics," in *Death and Dying in the Middle Ages,* ed. Edelgard E. DuBruck and Barbara I. Gusick (New York: Peter Lang, 1999), 315–16.

58. Reynolds, "Funeral Customs in Tolkien's Fiction," 50.

59. Primarily, this perception arises from the description of Aragorn's death; in his final moments, he surrounds himself with not only his son and his wife but his counselors and friends, making the Silent Street seem inhabited and accessible.

4. HAUNTING THE DEAD

1. Mike Parker Pearson, *The Archaeology of Death and Burial* (College Station: Texas A&M Univ. Press, 1999), 142.

2. John Blair, "Popular Culture in Late Anglo-Saxon Burial: An Ethnographic Approach," paper presented at the International Medieval Congress in Leeds, England, July 2006.

3. Victoria Thompson, *Boundaries in Early Medieval Britain* (Oxford: Oxford Univ. Press, 2003), 94.

4. Howard Williams, "Mortuary Practices in Early Anglo-Saxon England," *The Oxford Handbook of Anglo-Saxon Archeology,* ed. Helena Hamerow, David A. Hinton, and Sally Crawford (Oxford: Oxford Univ. Press, 2011), 240.

5. Linda-May Ballard, "Before Death and Beyond: Death and Ghost Traditions with Particular Reference to Ulster," in *The Folklore of Ghosts,* ed. H. R. Ellis Davidson and W. M. S. Russell (Woodbridge, Suffolk: Boydell & Brewer, 1981), 33.

6. Paul Barber, *Vampires, Burial, and Death: Folklore and Reality* (New Haven: Yale Univ. Press, 1988), 29–38.

7. Claire Russell, "The Environment of Ghosts," in Davidson and Russell, *Folklore of Ghosts,* 125.

8. Although it does not come first within the linear progression of the story, I start with the Passages of the Marshes because it is rooted in modern experience as much as medieval folklore. Within the chronology of the story, it is also the newest haunting. The Dead Men of the Mountains (also called the Shadow-Men, or simply the Dead) predate the ghosts of the Marshes only slightly, but from there, we shall move even farther back in time to the ancient legends encountered in the Barrow-downs. In all, these events mark the passing of more than six thousand years of imagined history.

9. J. R. R. Tolkien, to Professor L. W. Forster, Dec. 31, 1960, in *Letters of J. R. R. Tolkien,* ed. Humphrey Carpenter (New York: Houghton Mifflin, 2000), 303.

10. Nancy Caciola, "Spirits Seeking Bodies: Possession and Communal Memory in the Middle Ages," in *The Place of the Dead: Death and Remembrance in Late Medieval and Early Modern Europe,* ed. Bruce Gordon and Peter Marshall (2000; repr., New York: Cambridge Univ. Press, 2003), 66.

11. "Old Soldiers Never Die," *The Paranormal Database.* Jan. 22, 2007, http://www.paranormaldatabase.com/reports/battlefields.php?pageNum_paradata=3&totalRows_paradata=85; Marc Alexander, *A Companion to the Folklore, Myths, Customs of Britain* (Phoenix Mill, Gloucestershire: Sutton, 2002), 14.

12. Roy Palmer, *The Folklore of Warwickshire* (London: B. T. Batsford, Ltd., 1976), 20.

13. Alexander, *Companion to the Folklore, Myths, and Customs,* 59–60.

14. Mary L. Lewes, *Stranger Than Fiction: Welsh Ghosts and Folklore* (N.p.: Lethe Press, 2006), 106–7, 115–16. The Toili is a phantom funeral, linked to but not synonymous with the presence of the corpse-candle.

15. *Njal's Saga,* trans. Robert Cook (New York: Penguin, 2001), 130.

16. M. J. Walhouse, "Ghostly Lights," *Folklore* 5 (Dec. 1894): 295.

17. Tom Shippey, *The Road Goes Ever On: How J. R. R. Tolkien Created a New Mythology* (New York: Houghton Mifflin, 2003), 217.

18. Margaret Sinex, "Tricksy Lights': Literary and Folkloric Elements in Tolkien's Passage of the Dead Marshes," *Tolkien Studies* 2 (2005): 98.

19. Ibid., 93.

20. See Bede, *Ecclesiastical History of the English People,* book 4.8, trans. Leo Sherley-Price, ed. R. E. Latham (New York: Penguin, 1990), 218–20.

21. Jean-Claude Schmitt, *Ghosts in the Middle Ages: The Living and the Dead in Medieval Society,* trans. Teresa Lavender Fagan (Chicago: Univ. of Chicago Press, 1994), 124.

22. Walter Map, *De Nugis Curialium* [Courtier's trifles], trans. Frederick Tupper and Marbury Bladen Ogle (New York: Macmillan, 1924), 125–26.

23. These are found in the chronicle *Historia rerum Anglicarum* (1066–1198?), "William of Newburgh: History," vol. 2, book 5, chap. 6: 22–24, *Internet Medieval Source Book,* Aug. 2011, http://sourcebooks.fordham.edu/halsall/basis/williamof newburgh-five.asp. Most remarkably, some of the hauntings are given specific dates and places; the first, for instance, occurred in Buckingham two years before (1196). The same cannot often be said of most modern ghost stories, which tend to be told at some remove.

24. Nancy Caciola, "Wraiths, Revenants and Ritual in Medieval Culture," *Past and Present* 152 (Aug. 1996): 19.

25. Jacqueline Simpson, "Repentant Soul or Walking Corpse? Debatable Apparitions in England," *Folklore* 114 (2003): 396. For a transcription of the original (and rather bad) Latin, see M. R. James, "Twelve Medieval Ghost-Stories," *English Historical Review* 37 (July 1922): 418.

26. Hilda Roderick Ellis Davidson, "The Restless Dead: An Icelandic Ghost Story," in Davidson and Russel, *Folklore of Ghosts,* 174.

27. *Eyrbyggja Saga,* trans. Hermann Pálsson and Paul Edwards (New York: Penguin, 1989), 94, 140–41, 113.

28. Bruce Gordon, "Malevolent Ghosts and Ministering Angels: Apparitions and Pastoral Care in the Swiss Reformation," in *The Place of the Dead: Death and Remembrance in Late Medieval and Early Modern Europe,* ed. Bruce Gordon and Peter Marshall (Cambridge: Cambridge Univ. Press, 2000), 96.

29. Andrew Joynes, *Medieval Ghost Stories* (Woodbridge, Suffolk: Boydell, 2003), 29.

30. Ibid., 48, 49–53; see also Claude Lecouteux, *Phantom Armies of the Night: The Wild Hung and the Ghostly Processions of the Undead. [Chasses fantastiques et cohorts de la nuit au moyen age.]* 1991, trans. John C. Graham (Rochester, VT: Inner Traditions, 2011), 99–112.

31. Schmitt, *Ghosts in the Middle Ages,* 111.

32. "Manuscript E: Bodleian MS Laud 636," *The Anglo-Saxon Chronicle: An Electronic Edition,* vol. 5, literary edition, ed. Tony Jebson, last modified Aug. 17, 2007, http://asc.jebbo.co.uk/e/e-L.html. For a user-friendly modern English translation, see *The Anglo-Saxon Chronicles: The Authentic Voices of England, from the Time of Julius Caesar to the Coronation of Henry II,* trans. and collated by Anne Savage (London: Phoebe Phillips, 1982).

33. See John Lindow, "The Wild Hunt," in *Medieval Folklore: A Guide to Myths, Legends, Tales, Beliefs, and Customs,* ed. Carl Lindahl, John McNamara, and John Lindow (Oxford: Oxford Univ. Press, 2002), 432–33; "The Wild Hunt," in *A Dictionary of English Folklore,* ed. Jacqueline Simpson and Steve Roud (Oxford: Oxford Univ. Press, 2003), 390.

34. Kveldulf Hagen Gundarrson, "The Folklore of the Wild Hunt and the Furious Host," Lecture to the Cambridge Folklore Society, *Mountain Thunder* 7 (Winter 1992): n.p.

35. Map, *De Nugis Curialium,* 18; Lecouteux, *Phantom Armies of the Night,* 262.

36. Margaret Sinex, "'Oathbreakers, Why Have Ye Come?' Tolkien's 'Passing of the Grey Company' and the Twelfth-Century Exercitus Mortuorum," in *Tolkien the Medievalist,* ed. Jane Chance (London: Routledge, 2003), 160.

37. Alan Renoir, "The Heroic Oath in Beowulf, The Chanson de Roland, and the Nibelungenlied," in *Studies in Old English Literature in Honor of Arthur B. Goeder,* ed. Stanley B. Greenfield (Eugene: Univ. of Oregon Press, 1963), 242.

38. Douglas J. Canfield, *Word as Bond in English Literature from the Middle Ages to the Restoration* (Philadelphia: Univ. of Pennsylvania Press, 1989), xii.

39. John R. Holmes, "Oaths and Oath Breaking: Analogues of Old English Comitatus in Tolkien's Myth," in *Tolkien and the Invention of Myth: A Reader,* ed. Jane Chance (Lexington: Univ. Press of Kentucky, 2004), 250–51.

40. Wulfstan, *Sermo Lupi ad Anglos* [Sermon by Wulfstan to the English], in *Old and Middle English c. 890–c.1400: An Anthology,* ed. Elaine Treharne (Malden, MA: Blackwell, 2004), 228–29.

41. *The Battle of Maldon,* in *Old English Reader,* ed. Murray McGilvray (Peterborough, ON: Broadview, 2011), 67–77.

42. Fred C. Robinson, "God, Death, and Loyalty in The Battle of Maldon," in *J. R. R. Tolkien: Scholar and Storyteller: Essays in Memoriam,* ed. Mary Salu and Robert T. Farrell (Ithaca, NY: Cornell Univ. Press, 1979), 94, 95.

43. Ballard, "Before Death and Beyond," 39.

44. Joan Rockwell, "The Ghosts of Evald Tang Kristensen," in Davidson and Russell, *Folklore of Ghosts,* 53.

45. Schmitt, *Ghosts in the Middle Ages,* 104.

46. Theo Brown, *The Fate of the Dead* (Totowa, NJ: Rowman & Littlefield, 1979), 59.

47. Howard Williams, "Monuments and the Past in Early Anglo-Saxon England," *World Archaeology* 30 (June 1998): 104.

48. See Andrew J. Reynolds, *Later Anglo-Saxon England: Life and Landscape* (Stroud, Gloucestershire: Tempus, 2002), 110.

49. Elizabeth Jane Stern, *Legends of the Dead in Medieval and Modern Iceland* (Ann Arbor, MI: Univ. Microforms International, 1987), 57.

50. Malcolm Jones, "Barrows, Poems and Visions: The Inspired Dead," *Lore and Language* 15, nos. 1–2 (1997): 17.

51. Nora K. Chadwick, "Norse Ghosts II (Continued)," *Folklore* 57 (Sept. 1946): 106–27.

52. *Njal's Saga,* 130.

53. Victoria Thompson, *Dying and Death in Later Anglo-Saxon England* (Woodbridge, Suffolk: Boydell, 2004), 140.

54. Charles D. Wright, *The Irish Tradition in Old English Literature,* Cambridge Studies in Anglo-Saxon England (Cambridge: Cambridge Univ. Press, 1993), 258.

55. See L. V. Grinsell, "Barrow Treasure, in Fact, Tradition, and Legislation," *Folklore* 78 (Spring 1967): 1–38, esp. 1.

56. "The Tale of the Cairn-Dweller," in *The Complete Sagas of the Icelanders,* vol. 2 of 5, *Outlaws—Warriors and Poets,* ed. Karen Haber (New York: St. Martin's Griffin, 2001), 433–46.

57. Patrick Callahan, "Tolkien, Beowulf, and the Barrow-wights," *Notre Dame English Journal* 7 no. 2 (1972): 7.

58. Hilda Roderick Ellis Davidson, "The Hill of the Dragon," *Folklore* 61 (December 1950): 181.

59. *The Saga of the Volsungs,* trans Jesse L. Byock (London: Penguin, 1999), 59; "Gull-Þorir's Saga," in *The Complete Sagas of the Icelanders,* vol. 3 of 5, *Epics—Champions and Rogues,* ed. Viðar Hreinsson (Reykjavik: Leifur Eiríksson, 1997), 339.

60. "Gull-Þorir's Saga," 359.

61. Laurence K. Shook, "The Burial Mound in 'Guthlac A,'" *Modern Philology* 58 (Aug. 1960): 8.

62. *The Wife's Lament,* in *Old and Middle English Poetry,* ed. Elaine M. Treharne and Duncan Wu (Oxford: Blackwell, 2002), 22–25.

63. Sarah Semple, "A Fear of the Past: The Place of the Prehistoric Burial Mound in the Ideology of Middle and Later Anglo-Saxon England," *World Archaeology* 30 (Jan. 1998): 113.

64. Bruce Mitchell and Fred C. Robinson, *A Guide to Old English,* 6th ed. (Oxford: Blackwell, 2001), 265.

65. Old English nouns are inflected; *eorðscræfe,* which appears in the text, is the dative form. To parallel *morþor* and *eft,* I have used the nominative in this instance.

66. Tom Shippey, "Orcs, Wraiths, Wights: Tolkien's Images of Evil," in *J. R. R. Tolkien and His Literary Resonances: Views of Middle-earth,* ed. George Clark and Daniel Timmons (Westport, CT: Greenwood, 2000), 194.

67. Callahan may be referring to the possibility of Merry being possessed by the king's spirit when he says, "Merry's babbling expressed the presence of a consciousness not his own" ("Tolkien, Beowulf, and the Barrow-wights," 9). See also Verlyn Flieger, "The Curious Incident of the Dream at the Barrow," in *Tolkien Studies* 4 (2007): 110; Shippey, *Road Goes Ever On,* 110.

68. Paul Kocher, *Master of Middle-earth: The Fiction of J. R. R. Tolkien* (New York: Ballantine, 1972), 68.

69. J. R. R. Tolkien, *Return of the Shadow,* vol. 6 of *The History of Middle-earth,* ed. Christopher Tolkien (New York: Houghton Mifflin, 1988), 118.

70. J. R. R. Tolkien, "The Hunt for the Ring," in *Unfinished Tales* (Boston: Houghton Mifflin, 1980), 348.

5. APPLICABILITY

1. Joanne Lynn, introduction to *The Good Death: The New American Search to Reshape the End of Life,* by Marilyn Webb (New York: Bantam, 1997), xvii.

2. Kenneth Burke, *Philosophy of Literary Form* (Los Angeles: Univ. of California Press, 1967), 594, 296.

3. J. R. R. Tolkien to Mrs. Meriel Thurston, Nov. 9, 30, 1972, in *The Letters of J. R. R. Tolkien,* ed. Humphrey Carpenter (New York: Houghton Mifflin, 2000), 422, 423.

4. Renate Lachmann, "Cultural Memory and the Role of Literature," *European Review* 12, no. 2 (2004): 173.

5. Raymond Williams, *Marxism and Literature* (Oxford: Oxford Univ. Press, 1977), 12.

6. Jeff, Moore, "The Best Selling Books of All Time," Ranker.com, accessed May 15, 2017; http://www.ranker.com/list/best-selling-books-of-all-time/jeff419; "The Bible vs. Mao: A 'Best Guess' of the Top 25 Bestselling Books of All Time," Growth Markets, Sept. 7, 2010, PublishingPerspectives.com, http://publishingperspectives.com/2010/09/top-25-bestselling-books-of-all-time/; and The Statistic Brain Research Institute all agree on this number (presumably they are using the same source). In 2012, the *Guardian* published "The Top 100 Bestselling Books of All Time: How Does Fifty Shades of Grey Compare?" Aug. 9, Datablog, https://www.theguardian.com/news/datablog/2012/aug/09/best-selling-books-all-time-fifty-shades-grey-compare, which gave a far more conservative 967,466, but this figure includes only the United Kingdom, and one rather wonders how the publication came up with so precise a number.

7. See Michael D. C. Drout, "Introduction: Seeds, Soil, and Northern Sky," in *Beowulf and the Critics,* by J. R. R. Tolkien, ed. Michael D. C. Drout (2002;

repr., Tempe, AZ: Medieval and Renaissance Texts and Studies, 2005), 3. See also Douglas A. Anderson, "Tolkien after All These Years," in *Meditations on Middle-earth,* ed. Karen Haber (New York: St. Martin's Griffin, 2001), 140.

8. Tom Shippey, "Orcs, Wraiths, Wights: Tolkien's Images of Evil." In *J. R. R. Tolkien and His Literary Resonances: Views of Middle-earth,* ed. George Clark and Daniel Timmons (Westport, CT: Greenwood, 2000), 195.

9. Verlyn Flieger, *Splintered Light: Logos and Language in Tolkien's World,* rev. ed. (Kent, OH: Kent State Univ. Press, 2002), 160.

10. Tolkien to Michael Straight, Jan. or Feb. 1956, in *Letters,* 237.

11. For a more detailed discussion of Achilleus's decision and the reasons for it, see the first two chapters of Tod Lindberg's *The Heroic Heart: Greatness Ancient and Modern* (New York: Encounter Books, 2015).

12. Jocelyn Wogan-Browne, "The Hero in Christian Reception." In *Old English Literature: Critical Essays,* ed R. M. Liuzza (New Haven: Yale Univ. Press, 2002), 220.

13. Ernest Becker, *The Denial of Death* (1973; repr., New York: Free Press Paperbacks, 1997), 11–12.

14. Lance Kittleson, *Meditations from Iraq: A Chaplain's Ministry in the Middle East 2003–2004* (Lima, OH: Children's Sermon Service Publishing, 2005), 221–24.

15. Raymond Grant, "Beowulf and the World of Heroic Elegy," *Leeds Studies in English* 8 (1975): 67.

16. Diana Whaley, "Heroic Death in the Early Nordic World," in *Ritual and Remembrance: Responses to Death in Human Societies,* ed. Jon Davies (Sheffield: Sheffield Univ. Press, 1994), 171.

17. Clive Seale, "Heroic Death," *Sociology* 29, no. 4 (1995): 598.

18. Tony Walter, "Historical and Cultural Variants on the Good Death," *British Medical Journal* 327 (July 2003): 220.

19. D. B. Hogan and A. M. Clarfield, "Venerable or Vulnerable: Ageing and Old Age in J. R. R. Tolkien's *The Lord of the Rings,*" *Medical Humanities* 33 (Jun 2007): 5–10. See Halbert Weidner, *Grief, Death, and Loss: The Shadow Side of Ministry* (New York: Routledge, 2012), 67. See Yuri Bittar, Maria Sharmila Alina de Sousa, and Dante Marcello Claramonte Gallian, "The Aesthetic Experience of Literature as a Means for Health Humanization in Brazil: The Laboratory of Humanities from EMP (UNIFESP)," *International Journal of Health, Wellness, and Society* 3, no. 1 (2013): 25–42. This study was a fascinating program wherein participants read several classic novels, including *The Lord of the Rings,* to see if doing so would help them develop what one participant called an "amplified and human perspective" in the face of so much technology (33). Initial results strongly suggest that it did.

20. Kathleen Bokey and Garry Walter, "Literature and Psychiatry: The Case for a Close Liaison," *Australasian Psychiatry* 10 (Dec. 2002): 396, 397.

21. Arthur W. Frank, "Asking the Right Question about Pain: Narrative and *Phronesis*," *Literature and Medicine* 23 (Fall 2004): 214.

22. Nagraj G. Huilgol, "Myths," editorial, *Journal of Cancer Research and Therapeutics* 10 (Mar. 2014): 1.

23. Frances M. Boyle et al., "Multidisciplinary Care in Cancer: The Fellowship of the Ring," *Journal of Clinical Oncology* 23, no. 4 (2005): 916.

24. Amanda Howe, Nigel Smith, and Nick Steel, "'Doing' Quality: An Agenda for GP Leadership to Improve Patient Care," *Quality in Primary Care* 20, no. 5 (2012): 313–15.

25. Grant C. Sterling, "'The Gift of Death': Tolkien's Philosophy of Mortality," *Mythlore* 82 (1997): 16.

26. Rosemary Horrox, "Purgatory, Prayer and Plague: 1150–1380," in *Death in England: An Illustrated History,* ed. Peter C. Jupp and Clare Gittings (New Brunswick, NJ: Rutgers Univ. Press, 2000), 98.

27. Robert Halliday, "The Roadside Burial of Suicides: An East Anglican Study," *Folklore* 121 (Apr. 2010): 84.

28. Roy M. Luizza, "Beowulf: in Monuments, Memory, History," *Readings in Medieval Texts: Interpreting Old and Medieval English Literature,* ed. David Johnson and Elaine Treharne (Oxford: Oxford Univ. Press, 2005), 100.

29. Michael Welch, "The Mid-Saxon Final Phase," in *The Oxford Handbook of Anglo-Saxon Archaeology,* ed. Helena Hamerow, David A. Hinton, and Sally Crawford (Oxford: Oxford Univ. Press, 2011), 280.

30. Luizza, "Beowulf: Monuments, Memory, History," 96.

31. Paul Binski, *Medieval Death: Ritual and Representation* (Ithaca, NY: Cornell Univ. Press, 1996), 22.

32. Michael D. Higgins, "Of Myth-Making and Remembering," Keynote Address at the Theatre of Memory Symposium, Abbey Theatre, Jan. 16, 2014, Áras an Uachtaráin, http://www.president.ie/speeches/keynote-address-by-president-michael-d-higgins-at-the-theatre-of-memory-sy.

33. Richard E. Meyer, "'Pardon Me for Not Standing': Modern American Graveyard Humor," in *Of Corpse: Death and Humor in Folklore and Popular Culture,* ed. Peter Narváez (Logan: Utah State Univ. Press, 2003), 140.

34. Mike Parker Pearson, *The Archaeology of Death and Burial* (College Station: Texas A&M Univ. Press, 1999), 145.

35. Tolkien Society, "Peter Roe Memorial Booklets," *Peter Roe Memorial Fund,* 2017. http://www.tolkiensociety.org/society/publications/peter-roe/.

36. Kelvarhin, "In Memory of Shadowfax," *The One Ring,* Apr 6, 2014, http://www.theonering.net/torwp/2014/04/06/88420-in-memory-of-shadowfax/.

37. Baranduin, "Elanor of Westmarch: Grace," *Always Keep Ithaca in Your Mind.* Mar. 27, 2009. http://baranduin.livejournal.com/968811.html.

38. Burke, *Philosophy of Literary Form,* 297.

39. Frank McConnell, "You Bet Your Life: Death and the Storyteller," in *Immortal Engines: Life Extension and Immortality in Science Fiction and Fantasy,* ed. George Slusser, Gary Westfahl, and Eric S. Rabkin (Athens: Univ. of Georgia Press, 1996), 225.

40. Ibid., 224.

Bibliography

Alexander, Marc. *A Companion to the Folklore, Myths, and Customs of Britain.* Phoenix Mill, Gloucestershire: Sutton, 2002.

Anderson, Douglas A. "Tolkien after All These Years." In *Meditations on Middle-earth.* Edited by Karen Haber, 129–51. New York: St. Martin's Griffin, 2001.

Andersson, Theodore M. *The Growth of the Medieval Icelandic Sagas (1180–1280).* Ithaca, New York: Cornell University Press, 2006.

Andrén, Anders. "Places, Monuments, and Objects: The Past in Ancient Scandinavia." *Scandinavian Studies* 85 (Fall 2013): 267–81.

The Anglo-Saxon Chronicles: The Authentic Voices of England, from the Time of Julius Caesar to the Coronation of Henry II. Translated and collated by Anne Savage. London: Phoebe Phillips, 1982.

Ariès, Phillippe. *The Hour of Our Death: The Classic History of Western Attitudes toward Death over the Last One Thousand Years.* Translated by Helen Weaver. 1977. Reprint, New York: Barnes & Noble Press, 2000.

Atkinson, David William. *The English* Ars Moriendi. New York: Peter Lang, 1992.

Ballard, Linda-May. "Before Death and Beyond: Death and Ghost Traditions with Particular Reference to Ulster." In Davidson and Russell, *Folklore of Ghosts,* 13–42.

Barber, Paul. *Vampires, Burial, and Death: Folklore and Reality.* New Haven: Yale University Press, 1988.

The Battle of Maldon. In *Old English Reader.* Edited by Murray McGillivray, 67–77. Peterborough, ON: Broadview, 2011.

Beaty, Nancy. *The Craft of Dying: A Study in the Literary Tradition of the* Ars Moriendi *in England.* New Haven: Yale University Press, 1970.

Becker, Ernest. *The Denial of Death.* 1973. Reprint, New York: Free Press Paperbacks, 1997.

Bede. *Ecclesiastical History of the English People*. Translated by Leo Sherley-Price. Edited by R. E. Latham. New York: Penguin, 1990.

Bell, Suzanne. *Encyclopedia of Forensic Science*. New York: Facts on File Books, 2004.

The Beowulf *Manuscript: Complete Texts and* The Fight at Finnsburg. Edited and translated by R. D. Fulk. Cambridge, Massachusetts: Harvard University Press, 2010.

Binski, Paul. *Medieval Death: Ritual and Representation*. Ithaca, New York: Cornell University Press, 1996.

Bittar, Yuri, Maria Sharmila Alina de Sousa, and Dante Marcello Claramonte Gallian. "The Aesthetic Experience of Literature as a Means for Health Humanization in Brazil: The Laboratory of Humanities from EMP (UNIFESP)." *International Journal of Health, Wellness, and Society* 3, no. 1 (2013): 25–42.

Blair, John. "Popular Culture in Late Anglo-Saxon Burial: An Ethnographic Approach." Paper presented at the International Medieval Congress, Leeds, England, July 2006.

Bloomfield, Morton W. "Beowulf, Byrhtnoth, and the Judgment of God: Trial by Combat in Anglo-Saxon England." *Speculum* 64 (October 1969): 545–59.

Bokey, Kathleen, and Garry Walter. "Literature and Psychiatry: The Case for a Close Liaison." *Australasian Psychiatry* 10 (December 2002): 393–99.

Bonechi, Simone. "'In the Mounds of Mundburg': Death, War and Memory in Middle-earth." In *The Broken Scythe: Death and Immortality in the Works of J. R. R. Tolkien*. Edited by Roberto Arduini and Claudio A. Testi, 133–54. Zurich: Walking Tree Publishers, 2012.

Bourquin, Guy. "The Lexis and Deixis of the Hero in Old English Poetry." In *Heroes and Heroines in Medieval English Literature: A Festschrift Presented to André Crépin on the Occasion of His Sixty-fifth Birthday*. Edited by Leo Carruthers, 1–18. Cambridge: D. S. Brewer, 1994.

Boyle, Frances M., Emma Robinson, Stewart M. Dunn, and Paul C. Heinrich. "Multidisciplinary Care in Cancer: The Fellowship of the Ring." *Journal of Clinical Oncology* 23 no. 4 (2005): 916–20.

Brindley, David. *Richard Beauchamp: Medieval England's Greatest Knight*. Charleston, South Carolina: Tempus, 2001.

Brown, Theo. *The Fate of the Dead*. Totowa, New Jersey: Rowman & Littlefield, 1979.

Burke, Kenneth. *The Philosophy of Literary Form*. Berkeley: University of California Press, 1967.

Burns, Marjorie. "Bridges, Gates, and Doors." In *Perilous Realms: Celtic and Norse Mythology in Tolkien's Middle-earth*, 44–74. Toronto: University of Toronto Press, 2005.

———. "Night-Wolves, Half-Trolls, and the Dead Who Won't Stay Down." In Houghton et al., *Tolkien and the New Century,* 182–96.

Caciola, Nancy. "Spirits Seeking Bodies: Possession and Communal Memory in the Middle Ages." In Gordon and Marshall, *Place of the Dead,* 66–86.

———. "Wraiths, Revenants and Ritual in Medieval Culture." *Past and Present* 152 (August 1996): 3–45.

Callahan, Patrick. "Tolkien, Beowulf, and the Barrow-wights." *Notre Dame English Journal* 7 no. 2 (1972): 4–13.

Canfield, Douglas J. *Word as Bond in English Literature from the Middle Ages to the Restoration.* Philadelphia: University of Pennsylvania Press, 1989.

Caxton, William. *Here begynneth a lityll treatise shorte and abredged spekynge of the arte [and] crafte to knowe well to dye.* Westminster: 1490.

Chadwick, Nora K. "Norse Ghosts II (Continued)." *Folklore* 57 (September 1946): 106–27.

Christie, E. J. "Sméagol and Déagol: Secrecy, History, and Ethical Subjectivity in Tolkien's World." *Mythlore* 31 (Spring–Summer 2013): 83–101.

Clark, George. "Tolkien and the True Hero." In Clark and Timmons, *J. R. R. Tolkien and His Literary Resonances,* 39–51.

Clark, George, and Daniel Timmons, eds. *J. R .R. Tolkien and His Literary Resonances: Views of Middle-earth.* Westport, Connecticut: Greenwood, 2000.

Cohen, L. M. "Suicide, Hastening Death, and Psychiatry." *Archives of Internal Medicine* 158, no. 18 (1998): 1973–76.

Conrad-O'Briain, Helen, and Gerard Hynes. Introduction to O'Briain and Hynes, *The Forest and the City,* 13–18.

Conrad-O'Briain, Helen, and Gerard Hynes, eds. *J. R. R. Tolkien: The Forest and the City.* Portland, Oregon: Four Courts Press, 2013.

Croft, Janet Brennen. *War and the Works of J. R. R. Tolkien.* Westport, Connecticut: Praeger: 2004.

Daniell, Christopher, and Victoria Thompson. "Pagans and Christians: 400–1150." In Jupp and Gittings, *Death in England,* 65–89.

Davidson, Hilda Roderick Ellis. The Hill of the Dragon." *Folklore* 61 (December 1950): 169–85.

———. "The Restless Dead: An Icelandic Ghost Story." In Davidson and Russell, *Folklore of Ghosts,* 155–76.

Davidson, Hilda Roderick Ellis and William Moy Stratton Russell, eds. *Folklore of Ghosts.* Woodbridge, Suffolk: Boydell ⅂ Brewer, 1981.

Davies, Douglas J. *A Brief History of Death.* Malden, Massachusetts: Blackwell, 2005.

Davies, John, ed. *Ritual and Remembrance: Responses to Death in Human Societies.* Sheffield England: Sheffield Academic Press, 1994.

Dettman, David L. "Väinämöinen in Middle-earth: The Pervasive Presence of the Kalevala in the Bombadil Chapters of *The Lord of the Rings*." In Houghton et al., *Tolkien in the New Century*, 197–215.

Deyo, Steven Mark. "Wyrd and Will: Fate, Fatalism, and Free Will in the Northern Elegy and J. R. R. Tolkien." *Mythlore* 53 (Spring 1988): 59–62.

Dickerson, Matthew. *Following Gandalf: Epic Battles and Moral Victory in* The Lord of the Rings. Grand Rapids, Michigan: Brazos, 2003.

Drout, Michael D. C. "Introduction: Seeds, Soil, and Northern Sky." In *Beowulf and the Critics*. By J. R. R. Tolkien. Edited by Michael D. C. Drout, 1–29. 2002. Reprint, Medieval and Renaissance Studies 248. Arizona Center for Medieval and Renaissance Studies. Tempe, Arizona: Medieval and Renaissance Texts and Studies, 2005.

———. "The Tower and the Ruin: The Past in J. R. R. Tolkien's Works." In Conrad-O'Briain and Hynes, *J. R. R. Tolkien*, 175–90.

Drury, Susan. "Funeral Plants and Flowers in England: Some Examples." *Folklore* 105 (1994): 101–3.

Eyrbyggja Saga. Translated by Hermann Pálsson and Paul Edwards. New York: Penguin, 1989.

Flieger, Verlyn. "The Curious Incident of the Dream at the Barrow." *Tolkien Studies* 4 (2007): 99–112.

———. *Interrupted Music: The Making of Tolkien's Mythology*. Kent, Ohio: Kent State University Press, 2005.

———. *A Question of Time: J. R. R. Tolkien's Road to Faërie*. Kent, Ohio: Kent State University Press, 1997.

———. *Splintered Light: Logos and Language in Tolkien's World*. Rev. ed. Kent: Kent State University Press, 2002.

Frank, Arthur W. "Asking the Right Question about Pain: Narrative and *Phronesis*." *Literature and Medicine* (Fall 2004): 209–25.

Fry, Carol. "Two Musics about the Throne of Ilúvatar: Gnostic and Manichaean Dualism in *The Silmarillion*." *Tolkien Studies* 12 (2015): 77–93.

Gísli Sursson's Saga. In *The Sagas of the Icelanders*. Translated by Martin S. Regal. New York: Viking, 2000.

Gordon, Bruce. "Malevolent Ghosts and Ministering Angels: Apparitions and Pastoral Care in the Swiss Reformation." In Gordon and Marshall, *Place of the Dead*, 87–109.

Gordon, Bruce, and Peter Marshall, eds. *The Place of the Dead: Death and Remembrance in Late Medieval and Early Modern Europe*. 2000. Reprint, New York: Cambridge University Press, 2003.

Grant, Raymond. "Beowulf and the World of Heroic Elegy." *Leeds Studies in English* 8 (1975): 45–75.

Gray, Douglas. *Themes and Images in the Medieval English Religious Lyric.* London: Routledge & Kegan Paul, 1972.

Grettir's Saga. Translated and edited by Denton Fox and Herman Pálsson. Toronto: University of Toronto Press, 1974.

Grinsell, L. V. "Barrow Treasure, in Fact, Tradition, and Legislation." *Folklore* 78 (Spring 1967): 1–38.

"Gull-Þorir's Saga." *The Complete Sagas of the Icelanders.* Vol. 3 of 5, *Epics—Champions and Rogues.* Edited by Viðar Hreinsson, 335–59. Reykjavik: Leifur Eiríksson, 1997.

Gundarrson, Kvedulf Hagen. "The Folklore of the Wild Hunt and the Furious Host." Lecture to the Cambridge Folklore Society. *Mountain Thunder* 7 (Winter 1992): n.p.

Gusick, Barbara I. "The Ultimate Nothing: Death and the End of Work in Late-Medieval English Lyrics." In *Death and Dying in the Middle Ages.* Edited by Edelgard E. DuBruck and Barbara I. Gusick, 315–50. New York: Peter Lang, 1999.

Halliday, Robert. "The Roadside Burial of Suicides: An East Anglican Study." *Folklore* 121 (April 2010): 81–93.

Hanning, Robert W. "Prudential Penance." *Enarratio* 16 (2009): 14–42.

Harte, J. D. C. "Law after Death, or 'Whose Body Is It?' The Legal Framework for the Disposal and Remembrance of the Dead." In Davies, *Ritual and Remembrance,* 200–237.

Hill, John M. *The Anglo-Saxon Warrior Ethic: Reconstructing Lordship in Early English Literature.* Gainesville: University Press of Florida, 2000.

Hogan, D. B. and A. M. Clarfield. "Venerable or Vulnerable: Ageing and Old Age in J. R. R. Tolkien's *The Lord of the Rings.*" *Medical Humanities* 33 (June 2007): 5–10.

Holmes, John R. "Oaths and Oath Breaking: Analogues of Old English Comitatus in Tolkien's Myth." In *Tolkien and the Invention of Myth: A Reader.* Edited by Jane Chance, 249–61. Lexington: University Press of Kentucky, 2004.

Horrox, Rosemary. "Purgatory, Prayer and Plague: 1150–1380." In Jupp and Gittings, *Death in England,* 90–118.

Houghton, John Wm., Janet Brennan Croft, Nancy Martsch, John D. Rateliff, and Robin Anne Reid. *Tolkien in the New Century: Essays in Honor of Tom Shippey.* Jefferson, North Carolina: McFarland, 2014.

Howe, Amanda, Nigel Smith, and Nick Steel. "'Doing' Quality: An Agenda for GP Leadership to Improve Patient Care." *Quality in Primary Care* 20, no. 5 (2012): 313–15.

Huilgol, Nagraj G. "Myths." Editorial. *Journal of Cancer Research and Therapeutics* 10 (March 2014): 1–2.

Huizinga, Johan. *The Waning of the Middle Ages: A Study of the Forms of Life, Thought, and Art in France and the Netherlands in the Dawn of the Renaissance.* 1949. Reprint, New York: Anchor, 1989.

Huppé, Bernard F. "The Concept of the Hero in the Early Middle Ages." In *Concepts of the Hero in the Middle Ages and the Renaissance.* Edited by Norman T. Burns and Christopher Reagan, 1–26. Albany: State University of New York Press, 1975.

James, Montague Rhodes. "Twelve Medieval Ghost-Stories." *English Historical Review* 37 (July 1922): 413–22.

Johnson, David, and Elaine Treharne, eds. *Readings in Medieval Texts: Interpreting Old and Medieval English Literature.* Oxford: Oxford University Press, 2005.

Jones, Malcolm. "Barrows, Poems, and Visions: The Inspired Dead." *Lore and Language* 15 nos. 1–2 (1997): 15–22.

Joynes, Andrew. *Medieval Ghost Stories.* Woodbridge, Suffolk: Boydell, 2003.

Jupp, Peter C., and Clare Gittings, eds. *Death in England: An Illustrated History.* New Brunswick, New Jersey: Rutgers University Press, 2000.

Keister, Douglas. *Stories in Stone: A Field Guide to Cemetery Symbolism and Iconography.* New York: MJF Books, 2004.

Kieckhefer, Richard. *Magic in the Middle Ages.* 1990. Reprint, Cambridge: Cambridge University Press, 2003.

Kisor, Yvette. "'Poor Sméagol': Gollum as Exile in *The Lord of the Rings.*" In Houghton et al., *Tolkien in the New Century,* 153–68.

Kittleson, Lance. *Meditations from Iraq: A Chaplain's Ministry in the Middle East 2003–2004.* Lima, Ohio: Children's Sermon Service Publishing, 2005.

Klinger, Christopher A, Doris Howell, David Zakus, and Raisa B. Deber. "Barriers and Facilitators to Care for the Terminally Ill: A Cross-Country Case Comparison Study of Canada, England, Germany, and the United States." *Palliative Care* 28 no. 2 (2013): 111–20.

Kocher, Paul. *Master of Middle-earth: The Fiction of J. R. R. Tolkien.* New York: Ballantine, 1972.

Kreling, Barbara, Claire Selsky, Monique Perret-Gentil, Elmer E. Huerta, and Jeanne S. Mandelblatt. "'The Worst Thing about Hospice Is That They Talk about Death': Contrasting Hospice Decisions and Experience among Immigrant Central and South American Latinos with U.S.-Born, White, Non-Latino Cancer Caregivers." *Palliative Medicine* 24, no. 4 (2010): 427–34.

Lachmann, Renate. "Cultural Memory and the Role of Literature." *European Review* 12, no. 2 (2004): 165–78.

La Fontain, Jean. "Explaining Suicide: An Afterward." *Culture, Medicine, and Psychiatry* 36 (June 2012): 409–18.

Lecouteux, Claude. *Phantom Armies of the Night: The Wild Hung and the Ghostly Processions of the Undead.* *[Chasses fantastiques et cohorts de la nuit au moyen age.]* 1991. Translated by John C. Graham. Rochester, Vermont: Inner Traditions, 2011.

Lee, Christina. *Feasting the Dead: Food and Drink in Anglo-Saxon Rituals.* Woodbridge, Suffolk: Boydell, 2007.

Lewes, Mary L. *Stranger Than Fiction: Welsh Ghosts and Folklore.* N.p.: Lethe Press, 2006.

Lindberg, Tod. *The Heroic Heart: Greatness Ancient and Modern.* New York: Encounter Books, 2015.

Lindow, John. "The Wild Hunt." *Medieval Folklore: A Guide to Myths, Legends, Tales, Beliefs, and Customs.* Edited by Carl Lindahl, John McNamara, and John Lindow, 432–33. Oxford: Oxford University Press, 2002.

Luizza, Roy M. "Beowulf: Monuments, Memory, History." In Johnson and Trehearne, *Readings in Medieval Texts,* 91–108.

Lynn, Joanne. Introduction to *The Good Death: The New American Search to Reshape the End of Life,* by Marilyn Webb. New York: Bantam, 1997.

Map, Walter. *De Nugis Curialium* [Courtier's trifles]. Translated by Frederick Tupper and Marbury Bladen Ogle. New York: Macmillan, 1924.

McConnell, Frank. "You Bet Your Life: Death and the Storyteller." *Immortal Engines: Life Extension and Immortality in Science Fiction and Fantasy.* Edited by George Slusser, Gary Westfahl, and Eric S. Rabkin, 221–29. Athens: University of Georgia Press, 1996.

Meyer, Richard E. "'Pardon Me for Not Standing': Modern American Graveyard Humor." In *Of Corpse: Death and Humor in Folklore and Popular Culture.* Edited by Peter Narváez, 140–68. Logan: Utah State University Press, 2003.

Milton, John. *Paradise Lost.* Edited by Gordon Teskey. New York: Norton, 2005.

Mitchell, Bruce. "'Until the Dragon Comes' . . . Some Thoughts on Beowulf." *Neophilologus* 47, no. 2 (1963): 126–38.

Mitchell, Bruce, and Fred C. Robinson. *A Guide to Old English.* 6th ed. Oxford: Blackwell, 2001.

Mitchell, Stephen. "Memory, Mediality, and the 'Performative Turn': Recontextualizing Remembering in Medieval Scandinavia." *Scandinavian Studies* 85 (Fall 2013): 282–305.

Murray, Alexander. *Suicide in the Middle Ages.* Vol. 2, of 2, *The Curse of Self-Murder.* Oxford: Oxford University Press, 2000.

Njal's Saga. Translated by Robert Cook. New York: Penguin, 2001.

O'Brien O'Keefe, Katherine. "Heroic Values and Christian Ethics." In *The Cambridge Companion to Old English Literature.* Edited by Malcolm Godden and

Michael Lapidge, 107–25. 1991. Reprint, Cambridge: Cambridge University Press, 2005.

O'Connor, Mary Catharine. *The Art of Dying Well: The Development of the* Ars Moriendi. New York: Columbia University Press, 1942. Authorized facsimile by Ann Arbor, Michigan: University Microfilms, 1967.

Palmer, Roy. *The Folklore of Warwickshire.* London: B. T. Batsford Ltd., 1976.

Pearson, Mike Parker. *The Archaeology of Death and Burial.* College Station: Texas A&M University, 1999.

Plato. *Phaedo. The Great Dialogues of Plato.* Edited by Eric H. Warmington and Philip G. Rouse. Translated by W. H. D. Rouse. New York: New American Library, 1956.

Puhvel, Martin. "The Concept of Heroism in the Anglo-Saxon Epic." In *La funzione dell'eroe germanico: storicita', metafora, paradigma: atti del Convegno internazionale di studio, Roma, 6–8 maggio 1993.* Edited by Teresa Pāroli, 57–73. Rome, Italy: Calamo, 1995.

Purtill, Richard. *J. R. R. Tolkien: Myth, Morality, and Religion.* San Francisco: Ignatius, 1984.

Rateliff, John D. *The History of the Hobbit.* Part 1, Mr. Baggins. New York: Houghton Mifflin, 2007.

———. *The History of the Hobbit.* Part 2, *The Return to Bag-End.* New York: Houghton Mifflin, 2007.

Reimers, Eva. "Death and Identity: Graves and Funerals as Cultural Communication." *Mortality* 4, no. 2 (1999): 147–66.

Renoir, Alan. "The Heroic Oath in Beowulf, The Chanson de Roland, and the Nibelungenlied." In *Studies in Old English Literature in Honor of Arthur B. Goeder.* Edited by Stanley B. Greenfield, 237–66. Eugene: University of Oregon Press, 1963.

Reynolds, Andrew J. "The Definition and Ideology of Anglo-Saxon Execution Sites and Cemeteries." In *Death and Burial in Medieval Europe: Papers of the 'Medieval Europe Brugge 1997' Conference.* Vol. 2 of 11. Edited by Guy De Boe and Frans Verhaeghe, 33–41. Zellik, Belgium: I. A. P. Rapporten 2, 1997.

———. *Later Anglo-Saxon England: Life and Landscape.* Stroud, Gloucestershire: Tempus, 2002.

Reynolds, Patricia. "Funeral Customs in Tolkien's Fiction." *Mythlore* 72 (Spring 1993): 45–53.

Risden, Edward. "Plowing, Bowing, Burning, Journeying: Penance and Subverting Penance in Medieval Literature." *Enarratio* 16 (2009): 112–23.

Robinson, Fred C. "God, Death, and Loyalty in the Battle of Maldon." In *J. R. R. Tolkien: Scholar and Storyteller: Essays in Memoriam.* Edited by Mary Salu and Robert T. Farrell. 76–98. Ithaca, New York: Cornell University Press, 1979.

Rockow, Karen. "Funeral Customs in Tolkien's Trilogy." *Unicorn* 3, no. 1 (1973): 22–30.

Rockwell, Joan. "The Ghosts of Evald Tang Kristensen." In Davidson and Russell, *Folklore of Ghosts*. 43–72.

Russell, Claire. "The Environment of Ghosts." In Davidson and Russell, *Folklore of Ghosts,* 109–37.

Ryan, J. S. "German Mythology Applied: The Extension of Literary Folk Memory." *Folklore* 77 (Spring 1966): 45–59.

The Saga of the Volsungs. Translated by Jesse L. Byock. London: Penguin, 1999.

Saul, Nigel. *English Church Monuments in the Middle Ages*. Oxford: Oxford University Press, 2011.

Scheps, Walter. "The Fairy Tale Morality of *The Lord of the Rings*." In *A Tolkien Compass*. Edited by Jared Lobdell, 43–56. La Salle, Illinois: Open Court, 1975.

Seale, Clive. "Heroic Death." *Sociology* 29, no. 4 (1995): 597–613.

Semple, Sarah. "A Fear of the Past: The Place of the Prehistoric Burial Mound in the Ideology of Middle and Later Anglo-Saxon England." *World Archaeology* 30 (January 1998): 109–26.

Senior, W. A. "Loss Eternal in J. R. R. Tolkien's Middle-earth." In Clark and Timmons, *J .R. R. Tolkien and His Literary Resonances,* 173–82.

Schmitt, Jean-Claude. *Ghosts in the Middle Ages: The Living and the Dead in Medieval Society*. Translated by Teresa Lavender Fagan. Chicago: University of Chicago Press, 1994.

Scutts, Joanna. "Battlefield Cemeteries, Pilgrimage, and Literature after the First World War: The Burial of the Dead." *English Literature in Transition* 52 no. 4 (2009): 387–416.

Shippey, Tom. "Goths and Romans in Tolkien's Imagination." In Conrad-O'Briain and Hynes, *The Forest and the City,* 19–32.

———. "Orcs, Wraiths, Wights: Tolkien's Images of Evil." In Clark and Timmons, *J. R .R. Tolkien and His Literary Resonances,* 183–98.

———. *The Road Goes Ever On: How J. R. R. Tolkien Created a New Mythology*. New York: Houghton Mifflin, 2003.

———. "Tolkien and 'The Homecoming of Beorhtnoth.'" In *Roots and Branches: Selected Essays on Tolkien by Tom Shippey*. Edited by Peter Buchs, Thomas Honegger, and Andrew Moglestue, 323–29. Zurich: Walking Tree Publishers, 2007.

Simpson, Jacqueline. "Repentant Soul or Walking Corpse? Debatable Apparitions in England." *Folklore* 114, no. 3 (2003): 389–402.

Simpson, Jacqueline, and Steve Roud, eds. *A Dictionary of English Folklore*. Oxford: Oxford University Press, 2003.

Shook, Laurence K. "The Burial Mound in 'Guthlac A.'" *Modern Philology* 58 (August 1960): 1–10.

Sinex, Margaret. "'Oathbreakers, Why Have Ye Come?' Tolkien's 'Passing of the Grey Company' and the Twelfth-century Exercitus Mortuorum." In *Tolkien the Medievalist*. Edited by Jane Chance, 155–66. London: Routledge, 2003.

———. "'Tricksy Lights': Literary and Folkloric Elements in Tolkien's Passage of the Dead Marshes." *Tolkien Studies* 2 (2005): 93–112.

Spence, Lewis. *British Fairy Origins*. London: Watts, 1946.

Sterling, Grant C. "'The Gift of Death': Tolkien's Philosophy of Mortality." *Mythlore* 82 (1997): 16–18, 38.

Stern, Elizabeth Jane. *Legends of the Dead in Medieval and Modern Iceland*. Ann Arbor, Michigan: University Microforms International, 1987.

Sturluson, Snorri. *Edda*. Translated and edited by Anthony Faulkes. 1987. Reprint, North Clarendon, Vermont: Turtle Publishing, 1995.

"The Tale of the Cairn-Dweller." In *The Complete Sagas of the Icelanders*. Vol. 2 of 5, *Outlaws—Warriors and Poets*. Edited by Karen Haber, 433–36. New York: St. Martin's Griffin, 2001.

Thompson, Victoria. *Boundaries in Early Medieval Britain*. Oxford: Oxford University Press, 2003.

———. *Dying and Death in Later Anglo-Saxon England*. Woodbridge, Suffolk: Boydell, 2004.

Tolkien, J. R. R. *Beowulf: A Translation and Commentary*. Edited by Christopher Tolkien. New York: Houghton Mifflin Harcourt, 2014.

———. *The Book of Lost Tales*. Vol. 1 of *The History of Middle-earth*. Edited by Christopher Tolkien. New York: Houghton Mifflin, 1983.

——— *The Book of Lost Tales II*. Vol. 2 of *The History of Middle-earth*. Edited by Christopher Tolkien. New York: Houghton Mifflin, 1984, 247

———. *The Hobbit*. New York: Ballantine, 1966.

———. *The Letters of J. R. R. Tolkien*. Edited by Humphrey Carpenter. New York: Houghton Mifflin, 2000.

———. *The Lord of the Rings*. Reprint, New York: Houghton Mifflin, 1994.

———. *The Monsters and the Critics and Other Essays*. Edited by Christopher Tolkien. New York: HarperCollins, 1988.

———. *The Peoples of Middle-earth*. Vol. 12 of *The History of Middle-earth*. Edited by Christopher Tolkien. New York: Houghton Mifflin, 1996.

———. *The Return of the Shadow*. Vol. 6 of *The History of Middle-earth*. Edited by Christopher Tolkien. New York: Houghton Mifflin, 1988.

———. *The Silmarillion*. 1977. Reprint. Boston: Houghton Mifflin, 1998.

———. *The Shaping of Middle-earth*. Vol. 4 of *The History of Middle-earth*. Edited by Christopher Tolkien. New York: Houghton Mifflin, 1986.

———. *The Tolkien Reader*. New York: Ballantine, 1966.

———. *Unfinished Tales*. Boston: Houghton Mifflin, 1980.

Tyler, Susan, and Hillary Major. *The Early Anglo-Saxon Cemetery and Later Saxon Settlement at Springfield Lyons, Essex.* Chelmsford: Essex City Council, 2005.

Walhouse, M. J. "Ghostly Lights." *Folklore* 5 (December 1894): 293–99.

Walter, Tony. "Historical and Cultural Variants on the Good Death." *British Medical Journal* 327 (July 2003): 218–20.

Weidner, Halbert. *Grief, Death, and Loss: The Shadow Side of Ministry.* New York: Routledge, 2012.

Welch, Michael. "The Mid-Saxon Final Phase." In *The Oxford Handbook of Anglo-Saxon Archaeology.* Edited by Helena Hamerow, David A. Hinton, and Sally Crawford, 266–87. Oxford: Oxford University Press, 2011.

West, Richard C. "The Interlace and Professor Tolkien: Medieval Narrative Technique in *The Lord of the Rings.*" *Orcrist* 1 (1966): 26–51.

Whaley, Diana. "Heroic Death in the Early Nordic World." In *Ritual and Remembrance: Responses to Death in Human Societies.* Edited by Jon Davies, 165–85. Sheffield: Sheffield University Press, 1994.

The Wife's Lament. In *Old and Middle English Poetry.* Edited by Elaine M. Treharne and Duncan Wu, 22–25. Oxford: Blackwell, 2002.

"The Wild Hunt." *A Dictionary of English Folklore.* Edited by Jacqueline Simpson and Steve Roud, 432–33. Oxford: Oxford University Press, 2003.

Williams, Howard. *Death and Memory in Early Medieval Britain.* Cambridge: Cambridge University Press, 2006.

———. "Monuments and the Past in Early Anglo-Saxon England." *World Archaeology* 30 (June 1998): 90–108.

———. "Mortuary Practices in Early Anglo-Saxon England." In *The Oxford Handbook of Anglo-Saxon Archeology.* Edited by Helena Hamerow, David A. Hinton, and Sally Crawford, 238–65. Oxford: Oxford University Press, 2011.

Williams, Raymond. *Marxism and Literature.* New York: Oxford University Press, 1977.

Wise, Robert A. "The Things They Wrote." *New York Times,* March 21, 2004.

Wogan-Browne, Jocelyn. "The Hero in Christian Reception." In *Old English Literature: Critical Essays.* Edited by Roy M. Luizza, 215–35. New Haven: Yale University Press, 2002.

Wrenn, Charles Leslie. *Beowulf.* London: Harrap, 1973.

Wright, Charles D. "*The Irish Tradition in Old English Literature.* Cambridge: Cambridge University Press, 1993.

Wulfstan. *Sermo Lupi ad Anglos.* [Sermon by Wulfstan to the English.] *Old and Middle English c. 890–c.1400: An Anthology.* Edited by Elaine Treharne, 226–33. Malden, Massachusetts: Blackwell, 2004.

Index

Valar: "bad" death concept and, 36, 45; "good" death concept and, 16
Vercelli Book, 100

Walchelin (*Historica Ecclesiastica*), 92–93
Waldere (Old English poem), 14–15
Wales, "ghost lights" tradition of, 86
Wanderer, The (Old English poem), 68–69
Warwick, Earl of (Richard Beauchamp), 78
Wife's Lament, The (Old English poem), 102–5
Wild Hunt (*Petersborough Chronicle*), 93
William of Glos (*Historica Ecclesiastica*), 92–93

William of Newburgh, 90
Williams, Raymond, 3–4
Witch-King of Angmar, 14, 105
Withered Tree, 77–78
World Tree Yggdrasil (Old Norse mythology), 60
World War I, Battle of the Somme during, 83
Wormtongue. *See* Gríma Wormtongue
Wotan (pagan god), 92
Wulfstan of Ely (Archbishop), 95

yew trees, in cemeteries, 59–60
Younger (Sturluson), 61